ACHIEVING FACULTY DIVERSITY

DEBUNKING THE MYTHS

Daryl G. Smith

With Lisa E. Wolf and Bonnie E. Busenberg

Research Associates

Morgan Appel
Debbie Frazier Evans
Yolanda Rodriguez Ingle
Candace Introcaso
Daniel Martinez
Van Novack
Yolanda Robinson
Jake Rodriguez
Joy Rosenzweig

*The research in this report was assisted by grants from the Spencer Foundation
and the Ford Foundation. The data presented, the statements made,
and the views expressed are solely the responsibility of the author.*

Association of American Colleges and Universities, 1996

Published by
Association of American Colleges and Universities
1818 R Street, NW
Washington, DC 20009

Copyright 1996

ISBN 0-911696-68-7
Library of Congress Catalog Card No. 96-85493

Contents

1 Executive Summary

Contemporary observers of the American professoriate suggest that, with regard to relatively new faculty, two things are clear: (1) the current academic labor market provides few employment opportunities and (2) attempts to diversify the faculty continue to be one of the least successful elements of campus efforts to deal with diversity. While the failure of academic labor market projections has been the focus of much debate, the discourse on the diversification of the faculty has centered primarily on campus statements about the lack of scholars in the pipeline and the presence of bidding wars to attract faculty of color. Indeed, a report at a prestigious research institution about the university's diversity efforts stated this about achieving faculty diversity:

> Although a concerted effort has been made, small candidate pools and intense competition between top universities has made growth in faculty numbers extremely difficult. . . . In disciplines such as engineering, mathematics and many of the hard sciences, the number of qualified candidates is extremely limited. In 1989, for example, of the 393 doctorates awarded in mathematics to U.S. citizens, only six were earned by African Americans, eight were earned by Hispanics, while none were earned by Native Americans. Despite these problems, . . . commitment to diversification among the faculty has not lessened.

In contrast, many scholars of color and others have been critical of the lack of serious consideration given scholars of color in the hiring process, in part based on experiences which differ from campus rhetoric and perceptions about "bidding wars." This study was designed to investigate the reality of the experience of the labor market for new faculty, including faculty of color. The results describe the employment experiences of scholars who recently earned doctorates with funding from three prestigious fellowship programs. The sample group allowed reflection on the hiring process from a national lens, involved several hundred scholars of color from a variety of academic fields, and permitted control for the inevitable questions of quality.

PARTICIPANTS

Three hundred ninety-three recipients of Ford, Mellon, and Spencer fellowships who completed their Ph.D.'s since 1989 were invited to participate in extended telephone interviews about their job market experiences. Two hundred ninety-eight interviews (78 percent of the original sample) were completed. Of those interviewed, 26 percent were African American, 4 percent were Asian or Pacific Islanders, 35 percent were white, 32 percent were Latino, and 3 percent were American Indian. Approximately half of the sample were women. Fields of study included the humanities (43 percent), the social sciences (26 percent), the sciences (20 percent), education (4 percent), and fields related to ethnic and/or gender studies (4 percent).

PROTOTYPES

In order to adequately describe the job market experiences of the participants, eight prototypes differentiated predominantly by the degree of employment choice and type of position ultimately accepted, were developed. The figures in parentheses indicate the percent of the entire sample in each prototype.

Prototype 1: Sought after (9 percent)
Prototype 2: Good experience after applying (16 percent)
Prototype 3: Single but good choice (13 percent)
Prototype 4: Limited choice (9 percent)
Prototype 5: Took what they could get—the default
      (20 percent)

Prototype 6: Underutilized: No regular faculty appointment or equivalent (11 percent)

Prototype 7: Not faculty, but applied for faculty positions (6 percent)

Prototype 8: Not faculty, never applied for faculty positions (16 percent)

CONCLUSIONS

Overall, the subjects of the study are doing well. Most, regardless of race or gender, are in regular faculty positions (70 percent) or in postdoctoral positions appropriate to their fields (17 percent). Of those in faculty positions, 92 percent are in regular tenure-track positions or faculty posts at Ivy League institutions that do not have tenure. By and large, those who are now faculty members obtained their positions by traditional means: attending prestigious graduate institutions, delivering papers at conferences, and publishing. Their experiences contradict six myths currently prevalent about the academic labor market:

Myth one. Because there are so few faculty of color in the pipeline, they are being sought out by numerous institutions that must compete against one another in the hiring process.

Reality. The supply and bidding arguments are grossly overstated. Even in this highly select group of doctoral recipients, the difficulties of the job market and limited options affect most candidates. Theoretical frameworks that assume that supply and demand will predict an individual's experience were not supported by the study. Indeed, only 11 percent of scholars of color were in Prototype 1, and within gender and racial categories there was wide variation. One participant, a Latina, commented:

> I would say that I find it a little surprising that I do not regularly get phone calls with regard to recruitment. We are so few, it's amazing that most universities will say "We can't find anybody," yet persons like myself are not recruited. I think I should be getting phone calls, and I don't get phone calls.

Myth two. The scarcity of faculty of color in the sciences means that few are available and those that are available are in high demand.

Reality. The majority of scientists in this study (54 percent), all of whom are persons of color, were not pursued for faculty positions by academic institutions and continue to pursue postdoctoral study. Many scientists are quite concerned about finding jobs and others had already left academe for industry because of their inability to find positions.

Myth three. The kind of scholars represented in this study, both because of their competitive positioning in the market, and their elite education, are only interested in being considered by the most prestigious institutions, making it virtually impossible for other institutions to recruit them.

Reality. Our participants demonstrated a wide range of preference for desired positions, regions of the country, and institutional types. Some of these choices were based on limited mobility, but others were based on the environment the person wished to be in, a desire to teach a diverse student body, or the desire to be part of an institution that had a mission related to the individual's professional goals.

Myth four. Individuals are being continually recruited by wealthy and prestigious institutions having resources with which ordinary institutions cannot compete. This creates a revolving door that limits progress for any single institution in diversifying its faculty.

Reality. When people move, the reasons often focused on unresolved issues with the institution, dual-career choices, and questions of appropriate fit more so than on financial packages and institutional prestige.

Myth five. Faculty of color are leaving academe altogether for more lucrative positions in government and industry.

Reality. Choices to leave academe were as often a function of the problems of academe (such as the need to establish a career before the age of forty, inhumane search processes, and the difficult job market), as they were the result of irresistible temptations from the outside.

Myth six. Campuses are so focused on diversifying the faculty that heterosexual white males have no chance.

Reality. White men had a wide variety of experiences. While 20 percent were underutilized, 24 percent had a good experience in the labor market. In most of the cases where white men had difficulty finding a regular faculty appointment, the fields in which they specialized had virtually no openings. White men who had expertise related to diversity had a significant advantage on the job market.

OTHER CONCLUSIONS

1. Experience on the job market is affected by a number of important factors, including the kinds of scholarship a person pursues (new scholarship is particularly important); the degree to which a person is championed; and the complexity of adult lives, particularly that of two-career families.
2. Because of the limited job market in many fields, campuses have sufficient choice among applicants to be able to raise the level of requirements for qualified candidates, a serious disadvantage to those who attend less elite institutions.
3. The search and hiring process continues largely unchanged. The lack of diversity on search committees continues to limit the potential for introducing new perspectives to the process of evaluation.
4. There are key strategies that graduate institutions can use to encourage and nurture students in approaching the current market.
5. The primary goal of new scholars is to acquire a tenure-track position and achieve tenure so they can truly play a leadership role in their institutions by offering differing perspectives.
6. The climate for faculty of color in institutions remains uncomfortable and difficult, regardless of the circumstances under which the individual was hired.
7. Fellowships are important factors in fostering success, not only by providing financial support, but by facilitating the creating of networks.
8. Many scholars, regardless of gender and ethnic backgrounds, perceive that campuses are often more involved in talk than actions when it comes to diversity.

IMPLICATIONS

The current job market. There are fewer opportunities for faculty than had been predicted, although there is still the prediction of increased demand in the future. This study suggests that the opportunity for scholars of color will not necessarily grow with the shifting job market unless there are changes within institutional hiring practices to complement the demographic change in the pipeline.

Fellowships. Fellowships continue to be important but foundations might increase their effectiveness by building in more opportunities for past and present fellowship recipients to network.

Principles of good practice for hiring institutions. The study revealed some strategies, approaches, and attitudes that seemed to be the most effective for academic searches:

- Utilize networking to identify appropriate candidates
- Exert administrative leadership for diversity
- Cultivate institutional commitment to a diversified faculty
- Support affirmative action for the right reasons
- Address dual-career issues for candidates
- Provide posthiring support
- Avoid elitist, exclusionary thinking in hiring
- Champion desirable candidates

Principles of good practice for graduate institutions. The study also revealed strategies, approaches and attitudes of graduate departments that strongly affect the employment success of young doctoral recipients:

- Prepare students concerning employment opportunities and the management of the job search process
- Champion students in their job search efforts
- Keep students abreast of changes in their field
- Encourage the consideration of nonacademic careers

The Study

INTRODUCTION

Over the past two decades the academic labor market has behaved like a mirage in the desert. While new scholars were struggling through a difficult hiring environment, there was ever before them the illusion that in the near future conditions would ease. Forecasts in the early 1980s predicted an enormous demand for new faculty in the nineties as a function of increasing student enrollments and large anticipated faculty retirements. But as we now know, the financial retrenchment of the 1990s combined with the elimination of mandatory retirement has left higher education with relatively few openings in many fields. Still, some scholars continue to predict that the possibilities for new scholars will open up once again. These predictions also fueled the possibility that the faculty of the twenty-first century could finally achieve the diversity within its ranks that would reflect more closely the growing diversity within the student bodies of American colleges and universities. Unfortunately illusions, hope, and rhetoric often mask reality. In the mid-1990s most assessments of the condition of the professoriate suggest that the academic labor market continues to be very tight and that efforts to diversify the faculty continue to be one of the least successful elements of campus commitments to diversity.

Virtually every initiative concerning issues of diversity in higher education rests on the important task of diversifying the faculty. This task is important for a number of reasons: equity and social justice; providing faculty to serve as role models; the need to bring new scholarly perspectives to the curriculum and research; and the need to provide a variety of perspectives to institutional practice and decision making. As the enrollment in higher education becomes increasingly diverse, the imperative for faculty diversity grows more and more urgent. While there is evidence of increases in the diversity of faculty at the national level (Carter and Wilson 1994), and rhetoric to the contrary, most campuses have not been very successful in their attempts to attract and retain faculty of color (Blackwell 1988; Smith 1989; Washington and Harvey 1989; Wilson 1995; Yale University 1990; Strober et al. 1993).

In much of the literature, the primary concern about achieving true faculty diversity has centered on the relatively few faculty of color achieving doctorates. The assumption has been that achieving faculty diversity is hampered primarily by the absence of diversity in "the pipeline" (e.g., Clotfelter et al. 1991; Schuster 1992). A parallel assumption is that those faculty of color who seek academic posts are in great demand, are sought after, and are able to pick and choose academic posts. In spite of the current job market, the rhetoric has suggested that because of supply and demand, higher education's commitment to diversity means that there is a "bidding war" in which faculty of color are sought after over "traditional" white male faculty, who are hampered by the current shrinking set of opportunities. In this context, ordinary institutions believe they are not comparably rich enough, located well enough, or prestigious enough to attract the few candidates who are in such high demand (El-Khawas 1990; Harvey and Scott-Jones 1985).

An exhaustive search of the literature in higher education reveals a consistent set of explanations for the lack of diversity in faculty hiring based primarily on labor market theories of supply and demand:

1. There are limited numbers of faculty of color (the "supply argument"), as demonstrated by statistics citing the relatively few numbers of persons of color with doctorates in various fields, especially science and mathematics.
2. A bidding war exists that results from the high demand for faculty of color along with the limited supply. In this context, "ordinary" institutions cannot compete with wealthier institutions that are more attractive to the few candidates available and that are better able to provide monetary incentives.

In addition, a number of other propositions have been used to explain the lack of institutional success:

3. Faculty of color are leaving academe altogether for more lucrative positions in government and industry, with which higher education institutions cannot compete.
4. The turnover in faculty, once hired, is a response to more lucrative offers from prestigious institutions who lure faculty away from their current positions with money, research opportunities, more prestige, and better locations.

These propositions feed another widely held belief concerning the academic job market:

5. All institutions are so focused on diversity that being a white heterosexual male today is a major hindrance to finding an academic position, particularly given the difficult job market.

The bidding war and supply arguments and their correlates are offered over and over again to explain the lack of diversity in faculty hiring. At the same time, there is informal and anecdotal evidence to suggest that the hiring experience of faculty of color does not reflect these descriptions. Single job offers, lack of choice in where one goes, or underemployment seem to characterize this body of experience. These propositions call for empirically based analyses. Which of these conditions more adequately captures the employment experience of faculty of color? This report presents the results of a yearlong study that was designed to investigate the reality of the academic labor market experiences of new faculty, including faculty of color. What is the level of bidding? What factors influence the varied experiences of persons from different backgrounds and fields as they enter the job market?

These forceful views suggest that the lack of diversity in the faculty is a function of the hiring process and attitudes of institutions, not simply the limited number of faculty of color

BACKGROUND

These propositions, particularly the supply problem and the bidding war issue, are cited repeatedly in the literature and articulated on campuses as explanations for the inability to find, attract, and hire faculty of color (e.g., El-Khawas 1990; Harvey and Scott-Jones 1985). The first of these issues, the supply problem, is well documented in the literature. Relying primarily on the number of doctorates awarded by field each year, disaggregated by race and gender, there is consensus that supply is a problem. Indeed, there are ample data to support the statement that if all campuses were seriously trying to diversify their faculties, there would not be enough faculty of color to accomplish this at all thirty-five hundred institutions, or even all twenty-one hundred four-year colleges and universities, which presumably require faculty members to hold terminal degrees (Adams 1988; Bowen and Schuster 1986; Bowen and Sosa 1989; National Center for Education Statistics 1992; Thurgood and Clarke 1995).

Adding to the concern about supply have been numerous studies that look at the flow of doctorate recipients out of higher education into government and industry. Again, these studies tend to suggest that the increasing attractiveness of nonacademic careers is primarily an economic one, based on the availability of positions and the economic incentives in those areas (Brown et al. 1994; Bowen and Schuster 1986; Schapiro, O'Malley, and Litten 1991).

Indeed, labor market projections for faculty have relied almost entirely on economic theories of supply and demand. Because these econometric models have prevailed in much of the dominant higher education literature, the emphasis of policy and practice has been to increase the supply of faculty in the academic pipeline on the assumption that increasing diversity in the pipeline will naturally result in an increasingly diverse faculty. As a result, the primary focus of attention in recent years has been on efforts to encourage individuals to pursue academic careers (Adams 1988; Schuster 1992; Bowen and Schuster 1986; Bowen and Sosa 1989; Clotfelter et al. 1991; California Postsecondary Education Commission 1990; Myers and Turner

1995; Norrell and Gill 1991; Ottinger, Sikula, and Washington 1993; Solorzano 1993.) This emphasis on the "supply" problem has provided a ready explanation when search processes fail to find candidates that contribute to diversity.

The efforts to increase supply have been particularly focused in science and mathematics, where the data are particularly powerful concerning the lack of availability for faculty of color and white women (Golladay 1989; Ivey 1988; National Research Council 1991; National Science Foundation 1994; White 1989, 1992).

While it appears to follow logically that if faculty of color are in short supply, they must be in great demand, the presence of the bidding war paradigm has never been empirically substantiated beyond anecdotal evidence and the obvious bidding for certain well-known scholars (Mooney 1989; Olivas 1988; Suinn and Witt 1982; Wilson 1995; Yale University 1990). Indeed, this cause-and-effect relationship would only be true if the labor market were not impacted by factors outside supply and demand. In addition to a body of literature that has attempted to introduce factors that work against diversity in the faculty, many faculty, postdoctoral fellows, and administrators of color deny that the typical hiring experience of minority scholars is one of bidding wars. Rather, these individuals argue that the hiring pipeline for minority scholars is more likely characterized by underemployment or the same limited market experienced more generally. In addition, several academics have written articles that confirm the perceptions of the difficulties that minority faculty face and the presence of discriminatory hiring practices (Carter and O'Brien 1993; Almost no blacks 1994; Bronstein, Rothblum, and Solomon 1993; Collins and Johnson 1990; Cross 1994; de la Luz Reyes and Halcon 1991; El-Khawas 1988; Garza 1988, 1992; Menges and Exum 1983; Michelson and Oliver 1991; Moore 1988; Smith 1989; Staples 1984; Washington and Harvey 1989; Wilson 1987, 1995). These forceful views suggest that the lack of diversity in the faculty is a function of the hiring process and attitudes of institutions, not simply the limited number of faculty of color. Implicit in these explanations is the strong influence of race and gender in the hiring process.

Left in the wake of these competing perceptions of both theory and practice are the actual experiences of white men and women and the diversity of experiences among faculty of color. Here, the literature relies more on logical conclusions from the supply side argument, particularly given the difficult job market that is also acknowledged. The argument suggests that given the limited number of jobs available, and given the commitment of campuses to diversify the faculty, faculty of color and white women will have a significant advantage over white men in applying for any opening (Russell 1991; Sandler 1986; Shoemaker and McKeen 1975).

The higher education community needs to know more about the current job market for faculty, including faculty of color. Without new knowledge about the conditions in the academic labor market generally and experiences of individuals from a variety of backgrounds, perceptions held by academics and administrators of color will heighten anger and cynicism concerning the sincerity of higher education's commitment to diversity, and the myths about employment opportunities for all faculty will continue. At the same time, unverified beliefs that are held by faculty search committees may leave many campuses engaged in self-fulfilling prophecies regarding minority faculty recruitment (Opp and Smith 1994; Swoboda 1993).

METHODOLOGY

What characterizes the typical hiring experience for new faculty over the past five years? Is there really a bidding war for faculty of color? In the context of an admittedly tight job market, how do experiences differ by field, institutional background, gender, race, and ethnicity? These are the central questions addressed in this research study using both qualitative and quantitative analyses.

The study was designed to examine the experiences of scholars who had recently earned doctorates. Ford minority fellows, Mellon fellows, and a subset of Spencer fellows were included. These programs were chosen because they satisfy three important methodological criteria. First, these programs attract scholars of color and other scholars from across the nation and therefore allowed us to view the minority hiring process through a national lens, while simultaneously allowing us also to look at the hiring experiences of white women and men. Second, because these programs are fairly large, we could involve several hundred scholars of diverse backgrounds and from a variety of academic fields. This enabled us to get a broad picture of hiring experiences and issues. Third, because these programs are prestigious and competitive, requiring participants to undergo an initial screening process, we were able to respond to the inevitable questions of quality. This methodology, therefore, provides a conservative test of the hypothesis of the bidding war paradigm for faculty of color. This last point is very important. We expected that this pool of doctoral recipients should have had among the best experiences because they have been previously "labeled" as particularly successful and elite.

Three fellowship programs were included—Ford, Mellon, and Spencer. We attempted to include a panel of National Science Foundation (NSF) fellows to add to the study of scientists. There was, however, no access to the names and recent addresses of NSF recipients. The Ford fellowships include three separate programs focusing on support for underrepresented scholars of color during doctoral work, during the dissertation, or during the postdoctoral period. Awards are made for study in research-based doctoral programs in selected academic disciplines that will lead to careers in teaching and research at the university or college level. Eligible fields include behavioral sciences, humanities, social sciences, science, engineering, mathematics, and computer science. The selectivity varies from year to year and from program to program. In 1994–95 only one out of twelve applicants received funding.

The Mellon program supports the first year of doctoral work, funding humanists in the fields of cultural anthropology, history, political philosophy, music, literature, foreign languages, American studies, art history, philosophy, and religion. The ratio of applicants to awardees has been approximately one to ten.

The Spencer Foundation funds dissertation research related to education from any disciplinary perspective. The ratio of awardees to applicants is about one in twenty.

To answer the research questions, 393 Ford, Mellon, and Spencer fellows who had completed their Ph.D.'s since 1989 were invited to participate in the project. They agreed to submit to a thirty- to forty-five-minute telephone interview. All 217 Ford and 117 Mellon fellows from the relevant cohort were solicited. A randomly selected subset of 48 Spencer fellows was also included.

Interviews focused on the individual's experiences in the academic labor market, including: background characteristics, number of positions applied for, limits on the search process, number of interviews, job offers, and factors that may have helped or hindered the individual in the job market. Participants were also asked about whether they had the opportunity to negotiate packages, whether they saw institutions "bidding" for them, how seriously they were taken in the job market, and whether they had any advice to share with the higher education community on these issues. In addition, participants were asked to answer four Likert questions about whether they felt as though they were sought after, taken seriously, how their compensation package compared to others, and whether the work they were doing was what they had hoped to be doing when they finished their degree.

In addition to the qualitative analysis, some of the data were coded quantitatively to provide broad descriptive analyses and to provide the basis for some comparisons. Carnegie classifications were used to categorize institutional types for baccalaureate and doctoral degrees and for institution of current employment. In addition, whether these institutions were Ivy League, historically black colleges and universities (HBCUs), or women's colleges were also noted. Despite some use of quantifiable data, most of this research relies on qualitative analyses to capture the complexity of the experiences described by participants.

PARTICIPANTS

Out of 382 participants originally included, 299 interviews (78 percent) were completed. Table 1 reflects the response rate by fellowship program. Response rates for the Ford program reached 84 percent, 76 percent for the Mellon, and 58 percent for the Spencer. These differentials reflect, in part, the level of recent data kept by the sponsoring agency on fellowship recipients, since virtually no one refused to participate once contacted. In order to estimate response rates across racial and ethnic groups, further analyses were conducted based on the availability of initial information on race and gender. Relatively complete racial and ethnic data were available on the Ford Fellows. Table 2 reflects the participation rates by racial and gender groupings for that program. The participation rates ranged from 70 percent for African American women to 100 percent for Asian/Pacific Islanders and Native American women, the two smallest groups in the study. While we had no gender information from Mellon and Spencer, we could, at least, estimate gender breakdowns of the response rates for the Spencer and Mellon fellowships. Table 3 summarizes the participation rate by gender for the three fellowship groups. Overall, the participation rate for

Table 1. Response Rate by Fellowship

Total	Ford	Mellon	Spencer
78%	84%	76%	58%
n=299	n=182	n=89	n=28

Table 2. Response Rate by Race and Gender for Ford Fellows

	African American	Asian/ Pacific Islander	Mexican American	Native American	Puerto Rican
Male	86%	100%	84%	80%	95%
	n=31	n=1	n=32	n=4	n=18
Female	70%	100%	100%	100%	83%
	n=43	n=5	n=24	n=5	n=19

women was 78 percent and for men, 79 percent. The male response rate was lowered considerably by the 48 percent response for men in the Spencer Fellowship programs, even though these participants reflected only 13 percent of the initial group.

Table 3. Response Rate by Gender for each Fellowship				
	Total	Ford	Mellon	Spencer
Male	79% n=142	87% n=86	77% n=46	48% n=10
Female	78% n=157	81% n=96	75% n=43	67% n=18

There were 299 people in the final group of interviews, with 26 percent African American, 32 percent Latino, 35 percent white, 4 percent Asian/Pacific Islander, and 3 percent Native American. Table 4 provides the complete participation rate by the fourteen racial/ethnic and gender groupings employed in the study, while Table 5 reflects the ethnic breakdown for each of the fellowship programs. One can see the significant impact of the Ford program in developing scholars of color in these breakdowns, given the relative lack of diversity in the Mellon and Spencer groupings.

Table 4. Distribution of Sample by Race and Gender								
	Total	African American	Asian/ Pacific Islander	White	Native American	Puerto Rican	Mexican American	Other Latino
Total	100% n=299	26.1% n=78	3.7% n=11	34.8% n=104	3.0% n=9	12.3% n=37	18.7% n=56	1.3% n=4
Male	47.5% n=142	10.7% n=32	1.3% n=4	17.1% n=51	1.3% n=4	6.0% n=18	10.7% n=32	.33% n=1
Female	52.5% n=157	15.4% n=46	2.3% n=7	17.7% n=53	1.7% n=5	6.4% n=19	8.0% n=24	1% n=3

Table 5. Ethnic Breakdown for Fellowship Programs								
	Total	African American	Asian/ Pacific Islander	White	Native American	Puerto Rican	Mexican American	Other Latino
Ford	61% n=182	41% n=74	3.3% n=6	N/A	4.9% n=9	20% n=37	31% n=56	0% n=0
Mellon	30% n=89	1% n=1	3.3% n=3	92% n=82	0% n=0	0% n=0	0% n=0	3.3% n=3
Spencer	9% n=28	11% n=3	7.1% n=2	78.6% n=22	0% n=0	0% n=0	0% n=0	3.6% n=1

Table 6 summarizes the distribution of the years in which respondents completed their Ph.D.'s. Half of the sample received their doctorates in 1989, 1990, and 1991. While the average age was thirty-six, the ages of the sample range from twenty-seven to fifty-six. In the total group, 20 percent were in the sciences, 26 percent were in the social sciences, 43 percent were in the humanities, 4 percent in education, and 4 percent in fields related to ethnic and/or gender studies (Table 7). Table 8 reveals the proportion of the participants who had subfield specialties related to gender or ethnicity. Overall, 32 percent of the sample were in subfields related to ethnic studies and 14 percent related to gender studies. Thus, while few of the par-

Table 6. Distribution by Ph.D. Year						
1989	1990	1991	1992	1993	1994	1995
11% n=32	17% n=52	21% n=63	20% n=59	17% n=52	11% n=33	2% n=7

Table 7. Distribution by Field					
Science	Social Sciences	Humanities	Education	Ethnic/ Gender	Other
20% n=59	26% n=78	43% n=129	4% n=12	4% n=11	3% n=9

Table 8. Distribution by Subfield			
	Gender Field	Ethnic Field	Traditional Field
Yes	14%	32%	76%
	n=40	n=92	n=219
No	86%	68%	24%
	n=250	n=196	n=70

ticipants were located in ethnic studies or women's studies departments, well over one-third did serious work in these areas located within traditional disciplines.

In terms of their doctoral work, 93 percent of the participants attended Research I institutions, about 53 percent of which were public. Overwhelmingly, these were the elite Research I institutions such as the Ivy League schools, Stanford University, the University of California–Berkeley, the University of Michigan, and the University of California–Los Angeles. Indeed, almost one-third got their doctorates at Ivy League institutions. The distribution of bachelor's degrees was only slightly more diverse: 58 percent attended Research I institutions (one-third of which were Ivy League institutions), 16 percent attended Liberal Arts I institutions, 12 percent attended Master's I institutions, and the rest were spread among the other Carnegie classifications. Only ten (3 percent) attended HBCUs, and only ten attended women's colleges as undergraduates. Few attended Hispanic-serving institutions such as members of the Hispanic Association of Colleges and Universities. Given the relative potency of "special purpose" institutions in Ph.D. production, their underrepresentation in the pool of fellowship recipients should be noted.

3 Current Status and Experiences

A key question of the study relates to what these fellowship recipients are doing now. Overall, 70 percent of the entire group are currently in faculty positions, with 17 percent in postdoctoral appointments (mostly scientists), 5 percent in corporate positions, 2 percent unemployed, and 6 percent in a variety of other positions, including educational administration (Table 9). Of the 210 in faculty positions, 92 percent (192) are in regular tenure-track positions (Table 10). Not surprisingly, 90 percent of these relatively new scholars are at the assistant professor level and only 7 percent are tenured.

Table 9. Distribution of Sample by Employment				
Faculty	Postdoctoral	Corporate	Unemployed	Other
70%	17%	5%	2%	6%
n=210	n=51	n=14	n=5	n=19

Table 10. Tenure-Track Faculty or Ivy Faculty	
Yes	No
64%	36%
n=192	n=107

Table 11 provides a distribution of current employment by fellowship program. Because the Ford fellowship program is the only one of the three to fund science, it has a higher proportion in postdoctoral positions than otherwise might be true. The Spencers also support postdoctoral research. Nevertheless, 85 percent of the Mellons are in faculty positions—

Table 11. Distribution of Sample by Employment and Fellowship

	Faculty	Post-doctoral	Corporate	Unem-ployed	Other
Ford n=182	63% n=115	24% n=44	8% n=14	2% n=3	3% n=6
Mellon n=89	85% n=76	5% n=4	0% n=0	0% n=0	10% n=9
Spencer n=28	68% n=19	11% n=3	0% n=0	7% n=2	14% n=4

an impressive number considering the job market for those in the humanities. None are listed as unemployed. The combined number of Ford fellows in faculty and postdoctoral positions is 87 percent, with 8 percent in corporate positions and 2 percent listed as unemployed. Spencer fellows report 79 percent in faculty and postdoctoral positions, 14 percent in a variety of other fields including educational administration, and 10 percent (n=2) unemployed.

Table 12. Distribution of Sample by Employment and Field*

	Faculty	Post-doctoral	Corporate	Unem-ployed	Other
Humanities n=129	87% n=112	4% n=5	1% n=1	1% n=1	9% n=10
Social Sciences n=78	78% n=62	10% n=8	1% n=1	3% n=2	8% n=6
Science n=59	20% n=12	56% n=33	19% n=11	0% n=0	5% n=3
Education n=12	58% n=7	33% n=4	0% n=0	8% n=1	0% n=0
Gender/Ethnic Studies n=11	91% n=10	9% n=1	0% n=0	0% n=0	0% n=0
Other n=9	78% n=7	0% n=0	11% n=1	11% n=1	0% n=0

* Note 1 case missing field

Table 12 provides an overall distribution of current employment by primary disciplinary field. The table reveals that only the scientists were significantly present in the corporate world. Nineteen percent of the scientists are in corporate positions. Over half of the scientists are in postdoctoral positions and only 20 percent are in faculty positions. In contrast, well over two-thirds of the persons in all the other fields are currently in faculty positions.

From this purely quantitative perspective, this is a very elite group and, despite the job market, its members are, to a large degree, doing what they intended to do.

CURRENT SENTIMENTS

These young faculty members, no matter what job experience they had, indicated considerable satisfaction with their current job status. Certainly their responses to the question of whether they are doing what they had hoped, reflects this general satisfaction. Of all the participants, 85 percent indicated they are doing close to or exactly what they had hoped (Table 13), though 39 percent acknowledged being hindered by the job market. Evaluations of current employment situations ran the gamut from sincere enthusiasm to more cautious statements. Said one satisfied and

Table 13. Extent to Which Interviewees Are Doing What They Hoped			
Exactly	Close	Not Close	Far Away
39%	46%	7%	8%
n=114	n=135	n=20	n=24

sought-after candidate, "I think it's terrific. I basically could not be in a better job, in my opinion." A participant who had only a single but select job opportunity was equally ebullient: "I consider myself lucky. This is better than what I had ever expected to happen in terms of getting a job. . . . I look forward to coming to work each morning." A respondent who had only lim-

On the whole, participants with faculty
positions were highly positive about
their positions in the academy

---

ited job choices did not let that affect his reaction to the job he was able to
acquire:

> I love it. I love it. I'm in a place where my scholarly work is
> taken seriously and encouraged and where there is money
> for junior faculty research fellowships and where I can teach
> what I want to teach and where I can get involved in the
> life of the institution. . . . It's a phenomenal opportunity.

Said one sought-after participant:

> I'm satisfied. There's some programmatic things that I would
> change. . . . There's politics in every department but I have
> a lot of great colleagues here too. I'd say my working situa-
> tion is pretty positive. The pressure for tenure and publica-
> tions is intense everywhere, but I'm given a lot of support
> for that, both monetary and emotional.

Those with more difficult experiences offered positive but more cautious evaluations. A respondent with limited job choices stated:

> The work load is immense, but compared to the rest of the
> developed world, being a faculty member is a good deal. It's
> a job with a little bit of status. It's a pretty good situation
> and there are lots of benefits.

A young faculty member who had a single but select opportunity offered: "I enjoy teaching, I enjoy working with graduate students—the only
thing I did not expect was the burden of service, which was very heavy."

Many in our sample were finding that meeting the diverse expectations of an academic life was more challenging than they had anticipated.
As one African American woman who had had a limited choice of jobs
commented: "I'm overwhelmed right now because I'm doing course prep and

I'm trying to get my research established. There's a lot to do the first year in being an assistant professor and I'm feeling that." Another woman with a single but select opportunity said, "I feel like I have three full-time jobs in one right now. That is partly my own fault because I love to write and do research and then I have all these other responsibilities. . . . I am working on five hours of sleep a night right now."

Despite first-year acclimation anxiety, on the whole participants with faculty positions were highly positive about their positions in the academy. As one sought-after participant stated:

> I am doing what I wanted to do. I just didn't know what it
> meant to be an academic until I actually was one. . . . They
> don't teach us how to teach in graduate school, . . . don't
> tell you about the realities of academia. . . . All in all
> though, I am happy.

Surprisingly some people had experienced aspects of racism and sexism at their employing institution, but treated it with a philosophical attitude and remained basically positive about their positions. As one sought-after minority scholar put it, "I am probably in a fairly good position. I do teach what I want and design courses that feed into my scholarship and there is money for activities. . . . There is a lot of racism here, but there is a lot of racism everywhere." Another offered, "I am now in a position to make a difference in the lives of the ethnic minority students. But in terms of political, social and economic conditions, it's what I expected because of where I come from. I didn't expect to get treated like a colleague, but I wanted to." One Chicana scholar summed up the pragmatic attitude of many minority faculty in the following statement:

> I am doing what I wanted to do, researching and writing—
> in fits and starts, with agony, anguish and pain. . . . I don't
> think in my lifetime, as a woman, as a woman of color, as a
> Chicana, I will ever be comfortable in any department be-

"Without affirmative action, blacks will
not be invited to interview, and faculty
[will] not [be] present to change the scope
of the curriculum and faculty"

---

cause the issues are so monumental. . . . The department
right now, however, is a very congenial place.

We also heard, however, powerful statements about concern about
politics, the lack of support, and the lack of efforts to take individuals seriously once they were hired, particularly from persons of color. A faculty
member who left a traditional department for a more supportive environment in African American studies in another institution commented:

> People who have chosen this profession have committed
> themselves and offered their services to the profession and
> accordingly should be treated properly and respectfully. . . .
> I don't see that. I have become very critical of the university
> and the profession in general. I didn't know there was this
> baggage that came with the job. . . . I didn't know that the
> majority of this position had to do with fighting the system.

An American Indian who accepted an offer in psychology in the
Midwest says of her current experience:

> It's not bad. There are some pluses and minuses. I am a little
> tired of the politics. . . . I particularly enjoy my role with
> students. . . . If there is any reason to leave [it will be my
> husband's career]. His is best served on the East Coast so I
> may be on the job market again.

One African American scholar spoke with sadness of her present
working conditions:

> I find the current conditions of the college campus for black
> females appalling. We are still struggling with issues of di-
> versity because it does not exist. Without affirmative action,
> blacks will not be invited to interview and faculty [will] not

[be] present to change the scope of the curriculum and faculty. That saddens me.

Understandably, those participants who currently hold only temporary or part-time faculty positions voiced disappointment that they were unable to secure a tenure-track position. Still, though some were bitter, most seemed content with their current employment. The following quotations are representative of this group's views:

> My expectations did not exactly match what the outcome was. . . . Ideally, I would like to be on a tenure track and working teaching undergraduates, on a higher level than I generally am, and publishing. I realize that the longer I remain out in a nontenured position, the more limited my chances are of getting a job. I may very well have to consider other options. But right now I am content doing what I am doing.

> I envisioned myself in a tenure-track position, therefore my experiences has not measured up to my expectations. . . . I will probably be on the job market next year and if I can't find a position that offers some measure of security, I might consider leaving the field.

> I feel lucky, but also uncertain. [My contract is] not a sure thing. It's been renewed for next year, but that's the nature of the one-year contract. . . . I feel lucky to have gotten gainful and useful employment in the same institution as my wife.

The most bitter over their experiences on the job market were those individuals who were unsuccessful in their application for faculty positions and thus are not currently employed as faculty and who are not even in a comparable position in other settings.

> I am very bitter. I will go out on the job market one more
> year and if I don't get a job then I am leaving. . . . I have a
> lot of publications and it doesn't seem to do much good. It
> is not a matter of publish or perish. There just aren't any
> jobs, and departments are so confused about what they want
> that they just keep making strange hiring choices.

Certainly a sense of frustration was a lingering element in the interviews with such persons, but many seemed resigned to their situation. Said one, "I knew that when I started the job search process that it would be unlikely for me to get what I was trying for. I knew it wouldn't work out." Another stated, "With academic institutions, I haven't felt like I've gotten a fair deal yet. . . . But I am doing research and I'm doing what I trained to do. I feel very positive." Most seemed to be patient with the unfriendly job market and remained hopeful that the present situation would ameliorate and they would eventually find a tenure-track opening in their field.

> There is a lot of opportunity here [at the research institution]. I would like to get a position in a university teaching
> and researching and mentoring students for careers in science. I may have to change those plans drastically because
> of the job market, but I am going on the assumption that I
> will be able to get a job in a university.

Those who had applied for faculty positions but found something suitable outside of academe often remained committed to returning.

> When I started looking for positions, even though I considered industrial positions from the very beginning, I envisioned myself at this point being in an academic position
> somewhere. . . . I think I would like to be in academia at
> some point when the timing is right. I've always felt

strongly that I want to be teaching at a good school on my
own terms.

There were, of course, those who were pleasantly surprised when
they accepted a position outside of the university setting. Said one minority
scientist, "I am extremely pleased with my present position and I consider it
even better than an academic position." Another voiced this opinion: "I
love my current situation. I'm at a company that's growing. . . . I enjoy wak-
ing up in the morning and going to work."

There was a sense, however, with all these participants that they
would like to reenter the academy, if the opportunity presents itself and if
they can afford it.

> I want industrial experience and then I want to return to
> academia. But that's proving to be more difficult than I ever
> imagined. . . . I'm committed to return to academia with in-
> dustrial experience and give students a taste of what they're
> going for.

> I feel very positive. I feel that [accepting a job in industry]
> was the best decision I have made. I plan to try and get an
> academic position in the future.

> I am happy with my current job, making progress, getting
> recognition and promotions. I would consider academe
> again in the future, but wouldn't go in blind like I would
> have before. I would want to make sure it was a viable op-
> tion financially.

Postdoctoral fellows, particularly scientists, who have not yet applied for academic positions are cognizant of dual realities. The first is that
this is an extraordinary time in their career in which they have the luxury to
focus entirely on their research interests. As one Chicano plant geneticist

Universities often nurture inbreeding and specialize in producing duplicates of their professoriate, despite the fact that academe has a limited and ever-decreasing capacity to employ these reproductions

put it, "I really enjoy this [postdoctoral] job. I have very good colleagues, freedom and opportunity." The second is that it is useless to apply for jobs in their fields before one or two postdoctoral training periods are completed. Although for many young scientists this means an average of eight to ten years of intense work with very modest remuneration, few who had chosen this path spoke of any injustice or undue hardship associated with this system. A Puerto Rican woman in the field of neuroscience sums up the prevailing attitude:

> The postdoc period is giving me more liberty than I will ever have to do what I want in the lab. So I can enjoy the experience. Other people here are telling me to enjoy the postdoc because it is the best time I will ever have in the lab, and I am. I think it is true. I don't worry so much about how long it is going to take to get a position. People who go into this field know from the start they don't do this for the money. As long as we can work and be in something we want to do, then to me that is good.

Those respondents who never applied for faculty positions but do hold professional positions, often in industry, feel predictably satisfied with their choice. Some of these individuals did not want to submit themselves to the punishment of going into the difficult academic job market, but might still do it in the future if the market turns more favorable. Others, sensitive to the frustratingly modest pay scales at colleges and universities and long apprenticeship periods, opted for nonfaculty alternatives and are pleased with their choice.

> I did consider academics, I could have gone either way. But the work I am doing is very similar to the work I did when I was a graduate student, except at a faster pace. . . . Right now I am satisfied and from day one I have worked to make sure that I was being compensated adequately.

I think I've been extraordinarily lucky that I didn't have to
do three postdocs and I didn't have to fight my way through
a tenure-track position. I know a lot of people choose to do
that, but I look at my friends who graduated about when I
did and I feel really bad for them because you spend five
years getting a Ph.D. and then you do two to six years as an
apprentice and then you go to a job market that would offer
you less than you could have gotten if you'd gotten a two-
year M.B.A.

Graduate school focuses on the scholarly training of students and
often produces Ph.D.'s whose thinking about future careers is limited to the
classic professorial track. It is important to note that most participants in
this study who eschewed the academic world for a professional career in
business or industry are very happy with their choice.

I am doing better than I ever planned. I am so happy. I
think that I have started to see that there are a million
things that I can do. I have started to combine my doctorate
with things I have always wanted to do. I am in a great position and I can do whatever I want.

Universities often nurture inbreeding and specialize in producing
duplicates of their professoriate, despite the fact that academe has a limited
and ever-decreasing capacity to employ these reproductions. The unfortu-
nate narrowness with which many graduate students consider future careers
is more than adequately demonstrated in this survey by the fact that only
twenty-two (0.7 percent) respondents were found to be currently employed
professionally in industry without ever having applied for a faculty position.

Prototypes

SUMMARY

While almost everyone interviewed for the project commented on the extraordinary difficulties in the labor market, sometimes even citing the ways in which Bowen and Schuster's (1986) predictions have not come to pass, there was significant variation in the experiences of individuals. Discussing the labor market from the vantage of those interviewed depended on a number of parameters: geography, institutional preferences, year of the doctorate, and broad fields, as well as subfields. People reported their experiences in terms of which subfields were "hot" hiring fields in academe and during which years. Nevertheless, except for the science fields, which are quite different, the group as a whole is employed as faculty members.

Because the experiences of each individual were quite varied and complicated to describe, eight prototypes of experience in the labor market were developed to facilitate answering questions about how experiences differed. These eight prototypes focus on the primary questions of the study—the degree to which people experienced levels of choice and competition for their talents in getting their current positions.

The prototypes were developed after all the interviews were read and patterns in experience could be discerned. Then, each interview was placed in one of the categories. Following placement of all the interviews, each prototype was read to insure relative consistency within the category. In order to check for interrater reliability in the placing of individuals into prototypes, a random sample of 10 percent of the interviews were selected and rated by one other person. The interrater reliability was 93 percent. The eight prototypes which emerged from the data in this project are briefly described below. A more complete description of those in each prototype follows.

Prototype 1: Sought after. This category was created for those who had exhibited some of the experiences categorized in the literature as one of being "sought out" by institutions. This group received personal solicitations to apply for positions in addition to having a relatively high degree of success within the normal application process. These individuals tended to have a higher degree of choice in deciding where they wanted to work. There are a range of experiences represented by those grouped in Prototype 1. Some were recruited by a number of institutions, others were recruited by only one or two institutions. Some were offered every job they applied for, while others received offers from only one or two of the institutions where they were candidates.

Prototype 2: Good experience after applying. Individuals who conducted successful academic searches, had multiple offers, but who were not initially recruited fit into Prototype 2. An African American woman anthropologist, for example, applied for five positions and received three offers. Many of the individuals in this category were able to negotiate their packages to some degree and some were the beneficiaries of bidding wars. A white woman in English applied for thirty-eight positions and received three offers. She indicated that places tried to match the offers made by other institutions.

Prototype 3: Single but good choice. This category captures the experiences of those individuals who had only one choice of faculty position, but the choice was either their "ideal" position or was sufficiently desirable that the person felt pleased with the outcome. Often persons in this group were solicited for positions before they were fully in the labor market and were made an offer that was not in competition with any other offers. For example, an African American male in the humanities explained, "I wasn't looking for a job. This position came to me. I was asked to take a one-year position, temporarily for a faculty member that had gone on leave . . . he resigned the position . . . and basically they offered me the position."

Prototype 4: Limited choice. Persons grouped in Prototype 4 applied for faculty positions and received a limited number of offers—usually two—that were not their ideal choices. All of these scholars currently hold tenure-track faculty positions. An African American male psychologist is typical of this group: he applied for thirty academic positions and received two offers. Also typical is the experience of a white man in history who applied for fifty positions and received three offers. Only one of the offers was for a tenure-track position.

Prototype 5: Took what they could get—the default. Individuals in this prototype applied for faculty positions and only received one offer. In contrast to those in Prototype 3, the jobs offered to these individuals were not their ideal positions. These individuals had extremely limited options. Some of the individuals in this category applied for all relevant positions across the country, while others limited their searches in some way. Nonetheless, the outcome was that the person had no choice in position. For example, a Puerto Rican male biologist applied for five academic positions and received only one offer. It was from an institution at which he had worked part-time for several years while he was searching for full-time positions. Typical of the sentiments expressed by this group was the comment of a Chicano anthropologist who claimed, "I took what I could get." Similarly, an African American woman in religion commented, "I took it because I needed a job . . . the factor was unemployment."

Prototype 6: Underutilized: No regular faculty appointments or equivalent. Individuals in this category all sought out tenure-track faculty positions but only were able to get part-time faculty positions, temporary non-tenure-track faculty positions, or other positions which did not make full use of their academic work. Some of those in this category had to take administrative or postdoctoral positions as a stopgap measure. Many of the individuals in this category expressed frustration and are considering leaving academia.

Prototype 7: Not faculty, but applied for faculty positions. Persons in this category applied for academic positions but are currently not working as faculty members. These individuals fit into two broad categories: those

Several individuals noted that they might have
been able to negotiate even more if they had been
better prepared by their graduate programs about
the how-to of the academic labor market

---

that did not receive faculty offers and thus obtained an administrative or industry position, and those that received faculty offers but for whatever reason chose to pursue other employment options. Most of the individuals
grouped in Prototype 7 are not unhappy with their employment situations,
but most had planned on being in a tenure-track faculty position by this
point in their careers.

Prototype 8: Not faculty, never applied for faculty positions. Individuals in this category did not apply to academic positions and are therefore either working in postdoctoral positions or in industry. For many, especially those in science, the current expectation regarding the importance of
getting a postdoctoral fellowship before receiving a faculty position stopped
them from even applying. According to an African American male chemist,
"It is quite normal for persons in this discipline wishing to eventually work
in academia to find a postdoc." An African American woman added, "Nor-
mally biologists do postdoctoral work for five to seven years after their Ph.D.
before they get a permanent job." For this reason she did not apply for academic positions.

PROTOTYPE 1: SOUGHT AFTER

Prototype 1 individuals represent those sought out by the academic
world. Members of this group were actively recruited by institutions, were
asked to apply for openings, and were extremely successful in the academic
labor market, receiving multiple job offers. However, there was a range of
experiences represented within this prototype. Some individuals were offered every position to which they applied, while others received offers from
only a small percentage of institutions.

These participants were recruited by an average of three academic
institutions. It was atypical, however, for them to limit their search to such
recruiting institutions. Instead, individuals in Prototype 1 applied for approximately eleven positions each and were invited to five on-campus interviews. The average number of job offers for Prototype 1 was five—i.e., on
the average they received offers from every school at which they inter-

viewed. In considering this figure, it is important to remember that many of the individuals in this category withdrew from some of their searches after receiving viable offers from others.

More than one-half (57 percent) limited their search by geography or institutional type. In deciding which positions to accept, individuals in Prototype 1 were most likely to cite institutional location and institutional prestige as being important considerations.

One indication of the sought-after status of Prototype 1 respondents is that 96 percent of them indicated that they were able to negotiate their compensation package with their hiring school. While base salaries were often non-negotiable, most individuals in this category were able to negotiate improved working conditions such as reduced course loads, more leave time, and computers. Interestingly, several individuals noted that they might have been able to negotiate even more if they had been better prepared by their graduate programs about the how-to of the academic labor market. Furthermore, almost three-quarters of the individuals in this prototype (72 percent) stated that academic institutions were bidding against each other for their services. Bidding was most often orchestrated by the job applicant. As a sociologist explained, "If you get more than one offer . . . then you just take that information back and forth to the different departments and you try to then negotiate your contract according to the most desirable traits of each offer." About one-half of the sought-after individuals indicated that their compensation package was better than others in their academic fields; most of the rest indicated that their package was comparable to others in their field. Not surprisingly, this group felt relatively positive about their experiences on the academic labor market. In fact, only 8 percent of this group stated that they were hindered by a lack of available jobs. This figure is striking when compared to the 39 percent of the overall sample who volunteered that the job market itself hindered them.

Only twenty-seven individuals, less than one-tenth of the sample in this project, had experiences indicating a sought-after status in the academic labor market. Of all the ethnic minority women in this study, 14 percent were rated in Prototype 1. Of all the ethnic minority men, 9 percent were

When individuals in this prototype perceived
that an institution cared more about their
background than their abilities they were
likely to decline the academic position

---

rated as sought after. However, only 6 percent of all the white men and 4
percent of all the white women in the study had experiences which would
warrant their being rated as such.

The average age for the twenty-seven individuals in Prototype 1 was
thirty-eight, slightly older than the average for the total sample (thirty-six
years of age). For the most part, individuals in this prototype were educated
at the most elite institutions in the United States. One hundred percent
earned their doctorates from Research I institutions, with 28 percent graduating from Ivy League schools. It is not surprising, therefore, that the overwhelming majority of Prototype 1 (82 percent) believed that the reputation
of their Ph.D.-granting institution helped them on the academic labor
market.

Most of the sought-after indicated that they had made themselves
known in professional circles while they were in graduate school. In addition, approximately two-thirds stated that they had someone champion
their job search. However, it was a strong publication record which was the
most frequently cited factor used to explain the job market success of individuals in Prototype 1.

In this research project, success seemed also to be a function of field
of study. Tellingly, whereas almost 40 percent of those in Prototype 1 were
social scientists (11 percent higher than their representation in the whole
sample), there were no natural scientists in the group. Two-thirds of those in
Prototype 1 were in some type of ethnic-related field. This percentage was
much higher than that found in the total sample (32 percent). Those in
strictly traditional fields were underrepresented among members of this prototype. Almost four-fifths of those in Prototype 1 are currently employed at
Research I universities. The rest (about 11 percent) are employed at Liberal
Arts I institutions or at Research II institutions or at Doctoral Granting I institutions (11 percent). Academics in Prototype 1 were fairly satisfied with
their current academic positions. Approximately half of them stated that
what they were doing now was exactly what they had hoped to do. The
other half stated that their current employment situation was close to what
they had expected. While some individuals had complaints about their cur-

rent employment situations, most echoed the sentiments of a scholar who stated: "I am doing what I wanted to do. I just didn't know what it meant to be an academic until I actually was one. . . . All in all though, I am happy."

Diversifying the American faculty is an important issue to individuals in Prototype 1. Ninety-three percent indicated that they have observed campuses trying to diversify their faculties. However, almost one-fifth suggested that institutions are providing more talk than action in diversifying the faculty. For example, one academic in Prototype 1 stated: "The problematic issue is that institutions are doing it, not because they want to, but because they have to. . . . What is missing, and what would make this a smoother transformation is an ethical commitment to diversity." This sentiment was echoed by several individuals within this prototype. Interestingly, two-thirds thought that their race or ethnicity was helpful to them in their job search process. As one respondent stated, "It's a good time to be a woman of color on the academic labor market. I have no apologies. It's been a long time coming." According to another respondent, "Not just being a woman or a minority, but having a quality of scholarship and being a female minority makes you stand out." When individuals in this prototype perceived that an institution cared more about their background than their abilities they were likely to decline the academic position. As one woman stated, "I did not want to be selected because I was black. I wanted to be selected for the position because of my abilities. . . . Any signs that one is being hired for any other reason is an insult."

Two vignettes of individuals in Prototype 1 provide a more detailed description of their range of experiences. Professor A is an African American woman with a Ph.D. in religion and who specializes in African American women's history. She attended Ivy League institutions for both her graduate and undergraduate degrees. She is currently employed at her undergraduate alma mater in a tenure-track, full-time position. Professor A applied for six academic positions; two of these institutions sought her out and asked her to apply. She received two initial offers; she has received two additional offers since accepting one. In choosing her current position, Professor A considered location and also the institution's commitment to supporting

"At the moment, what I'm trying to do is to use those kinds of ways in which I'm being categorized so that I'm not reinforcing whatever crazy ideas that they have about diversity"

---

her field within the department and within the institution. She feels that the reputation of her graduate school and of her adviser helped her in getting her current position, as did the quality of her work. She also indicated that through her adviser she made "many, many, many connections before I finished my degree." Diversity is an issue of great concern to Professor A. She feels as though her racial background was helpful to her on the job market. When asked which factor was the most helpful to her in obtaining her present position, she answered, "I think they were looking for race and familiarity with the discipline." At the same time, she acknowledged that in trying to diversify the faculty, institutions can inadvertently tokenize people. She stated:

> The idea is that if you want a person of color, you create a job. If you want someone who is African American, you create a job in African American studies, and that's how you get them rather than trying to actively look for someone who works on Shakespeare who happens to be black. . . . Then what happens is, in my case, the tenure line for my job is special to my department because it was an attempt to hire a person of color. . . . This tends to create problems with other faculty members. They know I have access to tenure because of my background rather than because of my work.

She added that this special status is often difficult to deal with.

Professor B represents another example of a person in Prototype 1. She is an Asian American woman in the field of music. She went to large, public, research universities for both her Ph.D. and undergraduate degrees. Currently, she is a tenure-track assistant professor at a research university in the east. When she graduated with her doctorate, Professor B took a position at a prestigious liberal arts college. She describes the job market as "real tight" in her field and feels that she was lucky. During the last year of her dissertation work, Professor B applied for approximately twenty positions—

including both postdoctoral and academic ones. She did not limit her search in any way. Initially, she received only one academic offer—at the liberal arts college. After she had worked for two years, she was actively recruited by two other academic institutions. Both institutions invited her to campus for interviews and both offered her jobs.

Professor B's decision to leave the liberal arts college was based on three factors: (1) she liked the idea of being at a major research university and being able to concentrate on her scholarship; (2) she was attracted to the location of the other universities, which were in urban centers; and (3) she wanted to work with a scholar who was a star in her field and who was employed at the university recruiting her. In terms of what helped her get her present position, she feels that she was already active as a professional. She also stated that she is perceived as a good colleague. She added, "The kind of research that I do is seen as interesting because it expands boundaries." When asked about institutions trying to diversify the faculty, Professor B commented:

> In music departments which are traditionally aimed towards the Western canon, what they try to do is kill three birds with one stone if they possibly can. Not only do they get the non-Western world, but it's nice if they can get a woman in that slot, and it's even better if they can get a person of color in that slot. So that they can cover all of these bases with one little position.

She added that she finds this outrageous, but that she sees this happening again and again. She feels that her own ethnicity is not the only reason that she got these jobs. She commented, "I know I'm good at what I do. I love what I do. I know I do it well. At the moment, what I'm trying to do is to use those kinds of ways in which I'm being categorized so that I'm not reinforcing whatever crazy ideas that they have about diversity."

Very few Prototype 2's hold positions
which were specifically slated for a
woman or for a minority

PROTOTYPE 2: GOOD EXPERIENCE AFTER APPLYING

Prototype 2 can perhaps best be thought of as the classic model of employment for successful young members of the professoriate. The individuals grouped in this category did not receive solicitations to apply for academic positions. Rather, they proceeded with their job searches in the classic manner, finding out about openings in their field through professional publications and sending their resumes and letters of reference to appropriate institutions whose needs intersected with their interests and abilities. The average number of resumes sent out by members of Prototype 2 was twenty six. Inquiries typically yielded five to six campus interviews, which resulted in offers from approximately three of the schools originally applied to. The prestige of the school and its location were the most important factors these "classic academics" considered in deciding whether or not to accept an offer. There were few "bidding wars" among schools for the services of these qualified applicants. Less than one-half of the group experienced any type of counter-offering among prospective employers, and those that did reported such modest adjustments in original offers that it rarely entered their decision-making process. Although almost two-thirds of the group were able to negotiate some aspects of their initial contract, perquisites such as computers or release time were more likely to be successfully negotiated than any increase in entry-level salaries.

In this project's sample, Prototype 2 is composed of forty-eight individuals representing 16 percent of the total sample. The average age of members of the group is thirty-five. Almost equal numbers of men and women (twenty-five men and twenty-three women) were placed in Prototype 2. Twenty-one percent of all the white women in this study, 18 percent of all the white men in this study and 17 percent of all the ethnic men in this study had experiences in the academic labor market which placed them in the classic academic group. Only 12 percent of all the ethnic women in the study, however, followed the classic path in obtaining their initial academic positions.

The classic academics are an elite group. Virtually all of them (97.8 percent) received their doctorates from Research I institutions, almost one-half from Ivy League schools. It is not surprising, then, that most feel that the reputation of the school from which they received their Ph.D. helped them on the job market. Three-quarters of them made themselves known in professional circles while they were still graduate students and over 40 percent amassed creditable publication records in graduate school which they considered an important factor in their success on the labor market. Their hard work in graduate school earned them support when they went to look for professional positions. Almost two-thirds said that their job search was championed either by someone from their doctoral institution or by someone from the school to which they were applying. Prototype 2's are presently successfully employed at schools at which they really want to be working. Almost three-fourths of these employment schools are Research I universities, but only 12.5 percent are Ivy League institutions. Many in this group found themselves on the job market in 1989 through 1991, when employment conditions in many fields were not as constricted as they have been in the past few years. Others in this group commented that they were lucky and happened to enter the job market in a year when there were a significant number of good openings in their particular field.

Despite the fact that their paths to successful employment were traditional in every sense of the word, Prototype 2 classic academics overwhelmingly acknowledge the effort towards diversifying the faculty in today's colleges and universities and feel (whether they like it or not) that their ethnicity and/or their gender was helpful in obtaining their university positions. Very few Prototype 2's hold positions which were specifically slated for a woman or for a minority. Eighty percent reported that they primarily worked in a traditional field. Nonetheless, two-thirds of the group had done their dissertation on a gender-related or an ethnic-related topic and were qualified to teach in the emerging areas of ethnic and/or women's studies.

Stepping outside this composite drawing, detailed sketches of two typical members of the classic academic prototypes might be useful to help

Professor D felt disadvantaged as a white male as he started out, but less so at the end of his search. Not only does he believe he found an attractive position, but he also observed little ethnic diversity and only some greater gender diversity in his field

the reader capture the experience of this group. Professor C is an African American woman who received her Ph.D. in 1990 from an Ivy League school. Her field of study is English, her area of specialization is the literature of an early historical period. She has an appointment in the English department of a private Research I institution. She also teaches in the women's studies department. She went on the job market in a year when there was a good selection of openings in her area. Applying for thirty-four positions, she interviewed for fifteen, not on campus but at the annual Modern Language Association meeting. She received several offers from these interviews and two follow-up campus visits. Altogether she received five job offers and was able to negotiate salary somewhat at her top-choice school, although she found the process of negotiation quite stressful.

Professor C feels that it was her research, which she described as "cutting-edge," which helped her the most on the job market. On the other hand, she readily admits that her versatility was probably also a big plus. She had a good grounding in race and gender theory and could therefore teach both African American literature and women's studies courses. Professor C was exceptional in that she did not go to any professional conferences while she was a graduate student, but she spoke warmly of a champion at her doctoral institution who gave her advice concerning her job search and did mock interviews to help her prepare for the experience. Concerning the role which diversity played in her hiring, Professor C stated, "Of course part of me wanted to believe that my work was so good that everybody just wanted to interview me. But people were looking for African American faculty. . . . I got a sense though that places that interviewed me, for the most part, were legitimately interested in me." Although she had a good job market experience personally, from her subsequent participation on search committees Professor C feels that African American graduate students in general are shamefully neglected. As she put it:

> Graduate faculty assume that minority graduate students are
> going to get jobs so they neglect them in terms of prepara-
> tion and they don't do any work with them to make their

work the best it can be. They don't give them the advice
and guidance they need on the job market to present themselves well. . . . And people only trust a minority candidate
if they have been approved by an Ivy League institution.

Professor D, a white male, is also a member of the Prototype 2
group. He received his degree in religion from an Ivy League school and is
now an assistant professor in a religion department at a Research I institution. He does traditional research, specializing in biblical studies and an-
cient Middle Eastern religions. He found less than ten jobs in the year he
looked but had a choice between two attractive job offers. He felt that he
had a good experience because his research area offered literary as well as
scholarly merit. Like the majority in his cohort, he had made himself known
in professional circles while a graduate student. He was also championed by
his graduate adviser, who introduced him to a number of helpful people.
Professor D felt disadvantaged as a white male as he started out, but less so
at the end of his search. Not only does he believe he found an attractive position, but he also observed little ethnic diversity and only some greater gender diversity in his field.

PROTOTYPE 3: SINGLE BUT GOOD CHOICE

Prototype 3 is a category comprised of individuals who hold excellent jobs, but who entered these jobs through a set of circumstances which
circumvented a traditional job search. Although in many cases their options
were limited, these people were lucky in their employment experiences.
Many in Prototype 3, the "single but select" group, were never fully on the
job market. A few accepted temporary replacement positions while they
were "ABD" (all but dissertation) and had those positions turn into tenure-
track slots. Some who had dramatically restricted their search because of
family considerations or cultural ties to an area were fortuitously offered a
position which met their needs and accepted immediately. Included in this
subgroup are members of academic couples who refused to be separated geo-

Members of this group often described the job market at the time they got their jobs as very tough, discouraging, or abysmal, and were grateful they did not have to follow traditional paths to employment

---

graphically from their partners, Puerto Rican scholars who received their Ph.D. on the mainland but definitely wanted to return home to work, and an American Indian scholar who wanted to be near her tribe. Included in Prototype 3 as well are several Target of Opportunity appointments who had learned (from friends, mentors, networks) about openings at universities for minority candidates which were funded by special nondepartmental budgets. Frequently, these candidates had little or no competition in applying for their jobs. Others in Prototype 3 heard about excellent (traditional) openings before they had finished their dissertations, when they were not fully on the job market. Encouraged to apply (by a contact such as a Ford fellow at the school, by their dissertation adviser, by a dean, etc.), they accepted the offer extended to them, even though they were not fully on the job market, because it was simply too good to pass up. Included in this group are those individuals who did initiate a more traditional job search, but whose top choice came through so early that they withdrew their names from all other searches, without fully engaging in the other employment competitions. Members of this group often described the job market at the time they got their jobs as very tough, discouraging, or abysmal, and were grateful they did not have to follow traditional paths to employment. The average age of the group members was thirty-seven.

Of all the ethnic women in the study, 14 percent could be categorized as having experiences which place them in Prototype 3. Fifteen percent of all white women had similar experiences, as did 13 percent of all ethnic minority men. Only 8 percent of all white men, however, could be categorized in this prototype.

Prototype 3 members were unmistakably a select group. Ninety-five percent had received their Ph.D.'s from Research I universities, often from top-named schools, and over 40 percent had earned their doctorate from Ivy League schools. Not surprisingly, three-quarters of the group felt the reputation of their doctoral institution was a positive influence on their employment experience. Although more than 60 percent of Prototype 3's currently work at Research I universities (including 10 percent at Ivy League schools), 37 percent accepted positions at Research II, Degree II, Master's I, and Liberal Arts I institutions, often because they wanted to work at public schools with diverse student bodies. Approximately three-quarters of this "limited but lucky" group had written their dissertations on ethnic-related or gender-related topics and continued to work in ethnic-related or gender-related subfields at least for part of their research.

Because most of this group pursued a single opening to the virtual exclusion of others, there was limited opportunity to experience any type of bidding for their services. Although half were able to negotiate their original contract to include more favorable terms, modifications were moderate and adjustments to salary were the exception rather than the rule. Geographic location was the single factor which the majority of the group took into consideration in accepting their position. Almost one-half of Prototype 3 felt that the topic of their dissertation was of critical importance in obtaining employment. However, publications, mentoring, networking, and having been in some way previously known to the employing institution were also considered important. They are a professionally visible group, with almost 60 percent having made themselves known in professional circles while in graduate school. More than 50 percent of the group was championed in some way in their job search, but this represents ten percentage points less than those who were championed in Prototypes 1 and 2. The vast majority saw efforts towards diversification at colleges and universities, but a full 40 percent considered this lip-service only. About half thought that their own ethnicity had been a factor in obtaining employment and about half thought that their gender had been a factor. Almost everyone considered themselves lucky in having achieved exactly or close to what they wanted in an early career and in having done so not through a draining and highly competitive process, but through a set of fortuitous circumstances.

A good example of a member of Prototype 3 is Professor E, a female Pacific Islander in music who received her doctorate from a private East Coast institution. Her husband is also an academic who works in a related field. The job market is traditionally very competitive in her field and she was taking her time finishing her doctorate, doing research supported by

Fulbright fellowships, university fellowships, and Ford fellowships at the time that a unique job opportunity came to light.

A former Ford fellow working at a public West Coast Research I university wrote separate letters to this woman and her husband, asking them to apply for some Target of Opportunity positions which had become available at his institution. He felt that there were programmatic needs in music at his school that they could fulfill. He clearly championed their applications. The couple considered themselves extremely fortunate, applied to the university, and were awarded the positions. They did not try to negotiate their original contracts because they did not want to stretch their luck. Professor E is working hard now to achieve tenure because she realizes it will be extremely difficult to improve her situation. On the other hand, however, she does lament that "Those who get hired under affirmative action policies are forever tainted. You're here because you are an affirmative action hire. You didn't get the job because you earned it."

Another member of this group is Professor F, a Latino U.S. historian whose specialty is Mexican American history. A graduate of a prestigious private West Coast university, he benefitted from both a Mellon fellowship and a Ford dissertation grant and is now, after several years of teaching, utilizing a third independent award to complete a book. While writing his dissertation in 1992, Professor F realized that the job market was very tight and that there were very few openings for tenure-track positions available. He became aware of a newly created position in Chicano history at a midsize public institution in the west. The school is primarily undergraduate, but has a fine reputation. His graduate mentor heard about this position at a conference from a former graduate student now working at that western university. His mentor encouraged him to apply and the school, particularly the mentor's contact, was very receptive to his application. It was the only job Professor F applied for, and it was offered to him. He was able to negotiate his salary upwards a bit from the initial offer (he was an older candidate who had worked in education for a period before returning to pursue the Ph.D.). Professor F credits his success, both in returning to graduate school and in securing a good position, to support from the Chicano scholars' network. He acknowledges a great deal of talk about diversifying faculties, but thinks that constraints of funding are hindering the effort at public institutions. Moreover, he experiences resentment among faculty peers about efforts to diversify the institution, resentment often expressed in subtle ways.

PROTOTYPE 4: LIMITED CHOICE

Prototype 4 represents those individuals who obtained full-time, tenure-track faculty positions, but had a limited choice in selecting their position. Often these individuals had to select between institutions that did not represent their ideal jobs. This is a group which feels quite strongly that the academic labor market is very difficult. Almost half claimed that the job market itself hindered their ability to find an academic position. This percentage is considerably higher than the 38 percent of the total sample who felt this way. In fact, several individuals in this prototype mentioned applying for academic positions that disappeared off the market without being filled.

There were twenty-seven individuals in Prototype 4, representing 9 percent of the total sample. The average age of group members, thirty-six, mirrored the average age of the total sample. Equivalent numbers of men (fourteen) and women (thirteen) were categorized in this group. Similarly, there were not notable differences in the percentages of each race/gender group categorized as Prototype 4. Twelve percent of all the white men in this study, 6 percent of all the white women, 9 percent of all the ethnic minority men, and 10 percent of all the ethnic minority women were categorized in Prototype 4 because they faced limited choice in their job search experience.

The composite academic background of this group, while still stellar, demonstrated slightly more institutional diversity than was found in Prototypes 1, 2, and 3. Nonetheless, a full 93 percent of the scholars in this group earned their doctorates from Research I universities, and 30 percent attended graduate school at Ivy League institutions. Three-quarters of the individuals who had limited choice in their job offers still felt that the reputation of their graduate institution helped them in attaining their present position. Compared to the total sample, individuals in the social sciences were overrepresented in this prototype as were individuals in either ethnic-related or gender-related fields. Scholars in both the sciences and in humanities were slightly underrepresented in this prototype when compared to their proportions in the total sample.

On the average, scholars in Prototype 4 applied for twenty-six positions. About one-third limited their search in some way, usually by geographic location or family considerations. After applying they were invited to an average of four on-campus interviews and received an average of two offers, so they did have a choice of positions, although not their top choice positions. While two-thirds say they negotiated their compensation package at the hiring institution, they were more likely than the total sample to feel that their final compensation package was worse than others in their field.

Individuals in Prototype 4 credited their publications and award records and the presence of mentors with helping them to attain their current positions, rather than crediting their own efforts in making themselves known in professional circles. They were more likely than those in the total sample to say that someone, either in their graduate program or at the hiring university, had championed their job search. The factor that most hindered this group of scholars was considered to be the nature of the academic labor market itself.

Despite their struggles on the academic labor market, individuals in this prototype eventually found academic positions. Currently, they work in a range of academic settings. Approximately half are employed by Research I institutions; 15 percent are employed at Research II schools, 11 percent work at Doctoral Granting II and 11 percent are employed at Master's Granting I institutions. The remaining 10 percent work at either Doctoral Granting I or Liberal Arts I institutions. Only 7 percent work in Ivy League institutions. Over one-half of this group who experienced limited job choices indicated that they were doing exactly what they had hoped to do when they were in graduate school, although not at their top-choice institutions. An additional 37 percent stated that their current position was close to what they had initially hoped to be doing. This group did express concerns about the present state of higher education, however. Over one-third thought that their institution's efforts toward diversity were "more talk than action."

The experiences of Professor G are typical of those grouped into Prototype 4. Professor G is a white woman who earned her doctorate in religion from an Ivy League institution. She applied for seven academic positions while she was ABD and did not receive any offers. The following year she applied for twenty academic positions. In her words, "I applied for everything, even things I wouldn't have wanted to take." She was invited to two on-campus interviews during this round of applications, and both institutions subsequently offered her tenure-track positions. She describes the job market in her field as bad. She is satisfied with the institution that she chose but would like to be at a quality liberal arts school with a better library and a better location. She added that she doesn't anticipate that she will attain such a position. When asked whether she was doing what she planned to do with her degree, she answered, "I was trying to remain open-minded because there were so few jobs available."

Professor H's experiences were also typical of those in Prototype 4. H is an Asian American male who earned both his undergraduate and graduate degrees from Ivy League institutions. His field is American literature. He works at a research university on the East Coast and claims that he chose the position because of "the spouse thing." He explained that his wife was a faculty member at a nearby institution and that this job allowed them to coordinate their lives. Professor H describes the job market as "terrible" but added that "There were a number of jobs I could apply for which I considered to be decent." In attaining his current position, Professor H went on the job market three times. The first time, when he was also writing for a postdoctoral fellowship, he applied for three academic positions and received no interviews and no offers, but did get the fellowship. The next year, he applied to two schools and again did not receive any offers. At the end of his two-year postdoctoral fellowship he applied more widely, to about thirty schools. He was seriously considered by three of the institutions, but withdrew his applications once he was offered his current position. Professor H

Of particular interest to the findings of this study is that one-third of all the white men and one-third of all the white women were in a default position

credits his postdoctoral experience as being an immediate attraction to institutions during his third year of applying. Professor H is quite satisfied with his current employment but plans to keep an eye on the job market for dual-career prospects, since his wife is not in a tenure-track position.

PROTOTYPE 5: TOOK WHAT THEY COULD GET— THE DEFAULT

Prototype 5 could be considered a "default" group. They are employed in academia because they accepted the one offer which came their way, whether or not it met the criteria they had hoped for in employment. The jobs accepted by these individuals were usually not their ideal positions. Prototype 5 was the largest group in the taxonomy created in this report and included fifty-nine individuals, thirty men and twenty-nine women, who represented 20 percent of the entire sample. The average age of group members was thirty-five and one-half years. Of particular interest to the findings of this study is that one-third of all the white men and one-third of all the white women were in a default position; 16 percent of the ethnic minority men and 10 percent of the ethnic minority women were in the default academic position.

The default group members in Prototype 5 applied for jobs at times when the market conditions, both in general and specifically in their fields, were grim. Although half the group limited their search in some way, the average number of jobs applied for was approximately the same (twenty-seven) as the number applied for by members of Prototype 2, the classic academic group. Typically, default members received three campus interviews, but received only one offer.

The differences between members of Prototype 2, those who had a good experience, and members of Prototype 5, ones who took what they could get, are subtle. Fewer in the default group than in the classic academic group (89.7 percent as compared to 97.8 percent) received their Ph.D.'s from Research I institutions. Fewer of them (35.6 percent as compared with 45.7 percent) went to Ivy League schools for their doctorate. A much smaller percentage had focused their dissertation research on ethnic-related or gender-related topics (19.3 percent and 12.3 percent, respectively, in Prototype 2 as compared with 38.3 percent and 19.1 percent in Prototype 5) and only about one-third considered ethnic-related or gender-related concerns to be an area of their scholarly expertise as opposed to two-thirds who had this ability in Prototype 2. The topics of their dissertations were considered equivalently important by both groups in obtaining employment, but members of Prototype 5 had published less and had experienced less mentoring, networking, and past associations with the schools by which they were hired. Fewer had taken the time to become known in professional circles through attendance at conferences. More than 50 percent fewer members of Prototype 5 than members of Prototype 2 were championed in their job search. A full 60 percent of the default group blamed market conditions for their difficult experience, whereas only 17 percent of the classic academic group thought that it had hindered their search. Approximately one-third of the default group felt they simply were not prepared for being on the academic job market. An equivalent percentage of both groups reported seeing diversity efforts on campus, but many more default group members felt it was more talk than substance. About two-thirds (as compared with three-fourths of Prototype 2) felt that their gender and/or ethnicity had been somewhat helpful to them in seeking employment. Somewhat surprisingly, at least half of the default group said that their present position was at least close to what they had hoped for, and 34 percent reported that it was exactly what they had hoped for, indicating that 84 percent of the group was reasonably content in their employment. A 95 percent contentment rate was reported by those in Prototype 2.

A good example of Prototype 5 is presented by Professor I, a Chicana scholar specializing in comparative literature. She did her doctoral work at an Ivy League school and is now working at a large public Research I university in the Southwest, which she likes because of the ethnic diversity of the student body. She entered the job market in 1992–93, which she describes as a very bad year. Although she is a Chicana, her specialty is not Chicano/a literature. She applied to twenty-eight advertised positions before she finished her dissertation. She did not use her mentor or any networking to try to find a job. She received four interviews and was offered only one job, the one she is currently holding. She was not the school's first-choice candidate. Professor I had not been "pushed" to present at conferences and although her thesis readers wrote her good letters of recommendation, they did not take a more aggressive role in her search for employment. She feels that her employment school is trying to diversify its faculty and that her ethnicity ultimately helped her secure the position she holds. At the same time, she admits that her ethnicity may not have helped her employment endeavors in other places because her scholarly interests do not include ethnic studies. As a Chicana, she was advised by one of her professors not to go into African American studies, because the job market was likely to be inhospitable to her. She likes her job although she would prefer to be in New England for personal reasons.

Another who had a more difficult experience is Professor J, a white man in religious studies. He presently has a tenure-track assistant professorship at a regional university, but he was on the job market for three years before he secured that position. He applied for approximately twenty-five positions each of those three years. For the year after he received his degree, this scholar was forced to teach part-time and then took a one-semester replacement position. Having earned his Ph.D. from an Ivy League school, Professor J reports that it was psychologically very hard to fail at a job search, and that not enough students in his field realize that in the present academic employment climate it is common to do postdoctoral or part-time work before securing a tenure-track position. He used networking to a modest extent in trying to secure a position. Professor J was able to negotiate a starting salary increase of five hundred dollars (in lieu of moving expenses) with his hiring institution and negotiated a Tuesday/Thursday teaching schedule which allows him to comfortably commute on weekends to the home of his partner, some three-and-a-half hours away. During his graduate training, Professor J had not invested much time in attending conferences or becoming known in professional circles. He felt that his graduate school adviser not only didn't champion him, but kept the whole job search process at arm's length. He is not conscious of ever having lost a job because of ethnicity, gender, or sexual orientation. Although relatively pleased with his position, he feels he suffered psychologically before he secured it and urges that "truth in advertising" be emphasized between graduate faculty and their students. He feels strongly that students need to be told the reality of the job market early in their graduate studies.

PROTOTYPE 6: UNDERUTILIZED—NO REGULAR FACULTY APPOINTMENT OR EQUIVALENT

Individuals in Prototype 6 applied for tenure-track faculty positions, but currently hold either part-time positions, temporary non-tenure-track academic positions, or other positions which do not make full use of their academic background and accomplishments. Some of the members in the "underutilized" group had to take administrative positions or postdoctoral positions as a stopgap measure. Many of the individuals in this category expressed frustration and are considering leaving academia.

The thirty individuals in Prototype 6 represent 11 percent of the total sample. The average age for this group of scholars is thirty-five. Gender representation within the group is almost equal, with 54 percent (eighteen individuals) of the members being women and 46 percent (fifteen individuals) of the members being men. One-fifth of all the white men in this study held positions which underutilized their talents and education and thus were categorized in Prototype 6, but only 14 percent of the ethnic women, 8 percent of the white women, and 5 percent of the ethnic men found themselves in this situation.

Interestingly, individuals in this prototype were more likely than those in the total sample to have attended prestigious institutions as graduate students. One hundred percent earned their doctorates from Research I institutions (compared to 93 percent in the total sample), and 32 percent went to graduate school at an Ivy League institution (compared to 33 percent in the total sample). Sixty percent attended a Research I institution as an undergraduate (compared to 58 percent in the total sample), with 31 per-

Reflecting on the factors that helped them in
their job search, individuals in this prototype
most frequently credited previous association
with the hiring school

cent attending Ivy League institutions for their undergraduate degrees (compared to 20 percent in the total sample). A full 48 percent of members of
Prototype 6 were in the humanities, while 27 percent were in the social sciences and 21 percent were in the sciences. Interestingly, there was no one
from education and only meager representation from gender/ethnic fields in
this prototype.

On the average, those now employed in part-time, temporary, or
otherwise underutilized appointments applied for twenty-six positions, participated in an average of two on-campus interviews, but received only one
offer. Most were never in any way recruited by academic institutions and less
than 20 percent were able to negotiate their compensation packages in any
way. Fifty-eight percent described their compensation package as worse than
others in their field, while 37 percent claimed it was comparable to others in
their field. Half of the total sample in the study limited their search in some
way, and about half of those employed in temporary or part-time positions
did so. For a little less than half of those in temporary, part-time, or underutilized positions, that position was their only offer.

Reflecting on the factors that helped them in their job search, individuals in this prototype most frequently credited previous association with
the hiring school. Only 30 percent reported being championed in any way
and only 20 percent participated in a mentoring relationship. Overwhelmingly, the most frequently cited explanation for this group's lack of success in
the job search was the academic labor market itself. In fact, approximately
two-thirds of those employed in temporary or part-time positions claimed
that the market was a hindrance. Only 39 percent of the total sample voiced
such a feeling.

The majority (69 percent) of those in Prototype 6 stated that they
felt that institutions were attempting to diversify the faculty, but 44 percent
thought it was more talk than action. While 22 percent of this group
claimed that their ethnicity helped them on the job market (compared to
39 percent of the total sample), 28 percent claimed that their ethnicity hurt
them (compared to 14 percent of the total sample). Eighteen percent felt
their gender helped them, while 25 percent believed their gender hurt them.

Surprisingly, 20 percent of the individuals in this prototype reported that they were doing exactly what they had planned to do with their doctorates. Thirty-six percent of them described their situation as close to what they had hoped for. The remaining 45 percent described their situation as either not close to or far from what they had expected. A typical comment from an individual in Prototype 6 is as follows: "I thought I would be much further along professionally for my age. There aren't enough jobs in my field. . . . I'd be a lot happier if I had some sort of good permanent job somewhere. The notion of being uncertain in April and May and not knowing where I'm going to be and where I am going to teach is nerve-racking." Not surprisingly, this group of scholars expressed a high degree of frustration—many indicated that they would give the academic labor market one more try and then consider leaving academia. As one woman explained, "I realize that the longer I remain out in a nontenured position, the more limited my chances are of getting a job. I may very well have to consider other options."

When asked what they would like to say to the higher education community, the vast majority of individuals in this prototype expressed the sentiment that there were just too few jobs available—many recommended that graduate programs either shut down or slow the production of doctorates. A typical comment is as follows:

> There are too many people with Ph.D.'s . . . and there are not enough jobs. I don't see that this is going to change for many many years to come. . . . For departments to be expanding the number of Ph.D. candidates that they bring in, for departments to be starting up new Ph.D. programs when they used to only have master's, I think is difficult to justify because there is no place for the students to go.

The experiences of a Latino in geology who works as a senior research associate at a public research university is typical of that described by those in Prototype 6. Professor K earned his Ph.D. from a Research I institution in 1990. After graduating, he spent one year abroad and then spent one year working on his Ford postdoctoral fellowship. During that year, he applied for five faculty positions. In his words, he applied to "whatever jobs were in my field and in my subspecialty or were related to what I study." None of the tenure-track positions were offered to him, so he took the part-time position at the place where he had done his postdoctoral work. Professor K reports that he was an active participant in the major conferences in his field and that he had published a couple of papers by the time he received his Ph.D. When asked what hindered him in his job search, he claimed that the field was slow and the market was flooded with applicants. He plans to reenter the academic labor market after he builds up his publication record.

PROTOTYPE 7: NOT FACULTY, BUT APPLIED FOR FACULTY POSITIONS

Individuals in Prototype 7 applied for academic positions but are not currently working as faculty members. These individuals fit into two broad categories: those that actively pursued academic positions, did not receive faculty offers, but obtained comparable administrative or industry positions; and those who received faculty offers but, for whatever reason, chose to pursue other employment options. More than half of the members of the group indicated that despite their inability to get an academic position, they were doing either exactly or close to what they had hoped to do. But 41 percent of those in this category stated that their current employment situation was far from what they had initially hoped to be doing.

There are eighteen individuals in Prototype 7, representing 6 percent of the total sample. The average age of individuals in this group is thirty-five. Sixty-one percent of the membership in the group is male (eleven individuals), while 39 percent of the membership is female (seven individuals). Considering all the ethnic men in the study, 11 percent were categorized in Prototype 7. Six percent of all ethnic women in the study were placed in this group. But only 2 percent of all the white men and 2 percent of all the white women had labor market experiences which placed them in this category.

In terms of academic preparation, most (94.4 percent) of the individuals in Prototype 7 attended graduate school at a Research I institution; more than three-quarters (78.6 percent) went to a Research I institution as an undergraduate. An additional 14 percent earned their undergraduate degree from a Liberal Arts I institution. The proportion of those in Prototype 7 who attended graduate school at an Ivy League institution was lower than the percentage found in the total sample (14.7 percent compared to 33 percent).

Scientists, who make up 20 percent of the total sample in this study, made up half the membership of Prototype 7. Social scientists made up 17 percent of the membership; humanists and people in education fields made up 11 percent respectively; but those in ethnic or gender fields made up only 5.6 percent of the membership.

Individuals in Prototype 7 are currently employed in a variety of positions. Approximately one-quarter (23.5 percent) hold postdoctoral positions, over one-half (52 percent) work in corporations, and 6 percent are students. On the labor market, individuals in this prototype applied for an average of nineteen positions (both academic and nonacademic). They were not, for the most part, recruited by academic institutions. They typically went to one or two interviews and received one offer. Unfortunately, most of the respondents did not differentiate between the number of faculty offers and the number of nonacademic offers which they received.

In describing what helped them on their job search, the two most popular responses were having the opportunity to make oneself known in professional circles (63 percent) and the reputation of their graduate institution (65 percent). Compared to the 45 percent of the total sample who claimed that someone championed their job search, only one-quarter of those in Prototype 7 indicated that this was the case.

Scholars in Prototype 7 tended to feel that it was the lack of available jobs which hindered their job search the most. A higher percentage of those in this prototype expressed concern over the job market than did those in the total sample (50 percent compared to 39 percent).

Only 59 percent of the membership of Prototype 7 indicated that they had observed institutions attempting to diversify their faculties. Approximately half felt that this attempt was all-talk and little action, however. Only 6 percent of the group felt that their gender helped them in any way in the labor market, but more than one-third (35.3 percent) felt that it hurt them. In contrast 23.5 percent of the membership felt that their ethnicity was as asset, whereas 17.6 percent viewed it as a liability.

Dr. L is a good example of the individuals found in Prototype 7. He is a white art historian who earned his Ph.D. in 1992 from a major research university on the East Coast. He has applied for approximately six academic jobs a year since he graduated, and has received no offers. Since receiving his doctorate, Dr. L has held three prestigious postdoctoral positions and has been accepted for a fourth in the fall. Dr. L states that "it is typical for people in my field to do postdocs, but not typical for people to do four in a row." When asked what hindered him on the academic labor market, Dr. L explained, "The situation is terrible. There are far too many people with the degree. . . . I don't know anyone who was in my graduate program who has a tenure-track job. . . . There are so few jobs and so many applicants and the standards of hiring are so unclear that it is extremely discouraging."

Dr. L admits that he is bitter about his experiences on the academic labor market. He explained that he will try one more time to get a job and if unsuccessful, he will leave academia. He added:

> I understand that no one did it to me in the sense that people told me I would get a job . . . but I am not sure that it will happen and I am not sure that there is anything I can do to make it happen. It isn't a matter of effort, or talent, or attitude, or anything else. . . . It is not a matter of publish or perish—I have a lot of publications—there just aren't any jobs.

Dr. M, while also in Prototype 7, typifies a slightly different experience. Dr. M is an Asian American who earned a doctorate in philosophy in 1993. While finishing his dissertation, Professor M applied for twelve faculty positions in philosophy but withdrew his applications so that he could attend medical school. Describing the academic labor market in philosophy, he says it is "not that great. . . . There are always more applicants than positions." Though he had been accepted to medical school, Dr. M decided to apply for academic positions anyway. He stated, "If I got a really excellent job I might delay going to medical school." After interviewing for ten positions at the American Philosophical Association meeting, Professor M was invited to on-campus interviews at four institutions. After considering his options, he decided to withdraw his applications before any decisions were made and to pursue his medical degree. When asked to describe how he feels about his current employment situation, Dr. M stated, "I am content. . . . It is a difficult job taking care of sick people when you work so many hours. . . . But I could think of far less useful means of making a living." Dr. M was not at all bitter or upset about his current situation.

PROTOTYPE 8: NOT FACULTY, NEVER APPLIED FOR FACULTY POSITIONS

Prototype 8, defined as those who are not employed in faculty positions and have never applied for faculty positions, is made up of forty-nine individuals and represents 16 percent of the total sample. The prototype includes two disparate groups of individuals. More than half (62 percent) are postdoctoral fellows who feel that a postdoctoral experience is so critical to their professional training that they have not as yet applied for faculty positions, although they eventually intend to do so. The remaining 38 percent never applied for faculty positions after receiving their doctoral degrees and are currently employed in professional positions in industry, academia, or health-related fields. Of the thirty individuals who are postdoctoral fellows, twenty-six are scientists (including two M.D./Ph.D.'s who are currently doing their residencies). This means that of the total number of scientists (fifty-seven) contacted in this study, 46 percent are still in postdoctoral positions in universities, industrial laboratories, or hospitals. These postdoctoral fellows were awarded degrees between 1990 and 1994, the average year of

A few mentioned that academic salaries were simply not competitive and that they looked for professional positions so that they could pay off the debts they had amassed during their years of educational training

---

degree receipt being 1992. The period of postdoctoral training varies from individual to individual, but it is not unusual for it to be of four to six years duration, effectively lengthening the training time in science from the four or five years common in other disciplines to ten or eleven years. The effects of this extended training on scientists' experience in the academic labor market is discussed more completely in chapter 7.

Among members of Prototype 8 who were professionally employed in nonfaculty positions, five were employed as scientific researchers in private industry, two were academic administrators, one was a school psychologist and another was a clinical psychologist. Other occupations included a program officer at a private educational foundation, a freelance film producer, a lobbyist, a fair-housing investigator, and a research associate on an education project. The reasons given for not applying for faculty positions among the nonfaculty professionals varied. Some discovered during graduate school they were not interested in pursuing research and publishing as an integral part of their job and sought other options. Some had family or geographic restrictions on their employment. Cognizant of the difficult job market in academia, these individuals looked elsewhere for employment. Some, particularly those in applied research, were never interested in teaching and wanted to devote their energies entirely to research, which they could do in an industrial setting. A few mentioned that academic salaries were simply not competitive and that they looked for professional positions so that they could pay off the debts they had amassed during their years of educational training. As one African American sociologist put it:

> I'm not teaching now . . . because I have this incredible debt. It took me a long time to finish. . . . People can't afford to remain in academia. . . . I found myself approaching . . . middle age and basically looking for a career because the one for which I was trained I consider foreclosed.

In Prototype 8, the "postdoctoral and nonfaculty professionals" group, 59 percent of the membership is female, while 41 percent is male. Eighty percent of the category is made up of ethnic minorities, while only 20 percent of the members are white. The average age of the group is thirty-four.

From an educational standpoint, Prototype 8 is a slightly less elite group than many of the other prototypes. Only 85 percent of the members received their doctoral degrees from a Research I university (21.3 percent received it from an Ivy League school), and only 64 percent received their undergraduate degrees from Research I institutions (22 percent received their B.S. or B.A. degrees from Ivy League schools). Still, 71 percent felt that the reputation of their graduate institution was important for their obtaining subsequent employment.

For this group, as for most others, the location of employment seemed to be the most important limiting factor in the search for a job. Approximately one-third reported benefitting from the efforts of a champion in their quest for a position. An equivalent number reported benefitting from having a mentor during their graduate work. Although only half the group felt that they had had the chance to make themselves known in professional circles while in graduate school, this same half felt that being previously known to the company or university was very important in securing a position. Only one-third of the members of Prototype 8 felt that their previous publications had helped them and only one-quarter reported that networking had been very instrumental in their employment-seeking endeavors.

On the average, members of Prototype 8 applied for six positions and received one interview and one offer. Only one-third of group members were able to negotiate their initial salary and benefits contract in any meaningful way.

Half the group acknowledged that they were aware of discussions at institutions about taking action to increase diversity among faculty and students, but approximately one-fifth thought that these discussions amounted to little more than lip service. Only one-quarter of the group thought their gender had helped them in any way in their job search and one-quarter thought their ethnicity might have helped them in some way. Less than

"Most people in my field go on to do two postdoctoral fellowships and then find a tenure-track position in a university. They do not have the research support that I have, they do not have the salary that I have, and they do not have the responsibility I have"

10 percent thought that either their gender or ethnicity had negatively affected them in looking for a position. It is not surprising that very few of the postdoctoral and nonfaculty professionals in Prototype 8 had any interest in gender-related or ethnic-related subfields of their discipline or had written gender-related or ethnic-related dissertations.

A typical example of a postdoctoral member of Prototype 8 is Dr. N, a Puerto Rican scientist who works in the physics of vision. He is in the fifth year of a postdoctoral position at a university laboratory in the Northeast. He stated, "It is pretty essential in my field to have a postdoctoral experience. It helps give you the recognition and experience which will land you a good job. On the advice of my graduate adviser, I was only looking for postdoctoral positions." He is currently supported by a grant from the National Institutes of Health. When he looked for a postdoctoral position, he was looking for three things: a location within a reasonable distance from New York City where his wife had taken a job, a very good lab in his field, and a mentor who would take a vested interest in his welfare and progress. His adviser from graduate school (a Research II institution) championed his postdoctoral search and helped him search out the best places in vision research and made phone calls inquiring about postdoctoral positions. He had several possibilities, interviewed at six, and took the position he liked the best. Because of a fortuitous set of circumstances, his salary is approximately thirty thousand dollars per year, much better than the eighteen thousand dollars per year frequently earned by postdoctoral fellows. He considers the postdoctoral experience a wonderful opportunity to do research without any other requirements of regular faculty. Eventually, he plans to find an academic appointment and do research in vision. He admits that diversity was not at all important to him when he was looking for a postdoctoral position, and had nothing to do with his getting the position he wanted. But now that he is looking for an academic appointment, he really wants to work in a school which has a diverse student body and a diverse faculty. He notes the following about his present situation:

Until two years ago the division I work in was all white
males over forty. Now they have two white males who are in
their thirties. They have a fair number of women graduate
and undergraduate students, but very few who are minorities. . . . Among the graduate students, there are several
Americans, some Canadians, several Chinese and Japanese,
and there are no Hispanics or blacks. It would be nice to
have other faculty of color in the department. . . . It is a social aspect. Sometimes one would just like to speak one's
language or meet people with similar backgrounds, just be
yourself. Comfort is simply not there right now.

Typical of the nonfaculty professionals in Prototype 8 is Dr. O, an
American Indian woman who is a director of a private molecular biology
laboratory. She worked in cancer research for her doctorate and knew she
wanted to continue. She did not want to leave her home state because of
her husband's employment and because of her own personal ties there. She
learned about her present position while a postdoctoral fellow doing cancer
research in a university laboratory. A private laboratory which did similar
research approached her with a job offer even though she wasn't really on
the job market. Although she was solicited for a few academic positions, she
did not take the solicitations seriously. She feels that the compensation
package she enjoys in her present position is a lot better than others in her
field "because most people in my field go on to do two postdoctoral fellowships and then . . . find a tenure-track position in a university. . . . They do
not have the research support that I have, they do not have the salary that I
have, and they do not have the responsibility I have." Both her Ph.D. adviser and her postdoctoral adviser championed her cause in obtaining this
industrial position. She feels that ethnicity and gender is a factor in every
job search, and feels that women in science are not taken as seriously as
men. Dr. O intends to stay in industrial positions, probably in biotechnol-
ogy, and is not tempted to return to an academic setting. As she puts it:

I think that I have been extraordinarily lucky that I didn't have to do three postdocs and I didn't have to fight my way through a tenure-track position. I know a lot of people choose to do that, but I look at my friends who graduated about when I did and I feel really bad for them because you spend five years getting a Ph.D., and then you do two to six years as . . . an apprentice [postdoctoral fellow] and then you go to a job market that would offer you less than what you could have gotten if you'd gotten a two-year M.B.A. I think that the value that Americans put on scientific knowledge is way too low.

5 Experiences by Race and Gender

A key question of this study was how does the experience in the labor market, (as characterized by these eight prototypes) vary by race and gender? Table 14 includes the distribution among the prototypes for the four major race and gender clusters.

Table 14. Prototypes by Major Race/Ethnic Groupings					
Prototype	White Men	White Women	Ethnic Men	Ethnic Women	Row Total
1	3 6%	2 4%	8 9%	14 14%	27 9%
2	9 18%	11 21%	16 18%	12 12%	48 16%
3	4 8%	8 15%	12 13%	14 14%	38 13%
4	6 12%	3 6%	8 9%	10 10%	27 9%
5	16 31%	16 30%	14 15%	13 13%	59 20%
6	10 20%	4 8%	5 6%	14 14%	33 11%
7	1 2%	1 2%	10 11%	6 6%	18 6%
8	2 4%	8 15%	18 20%	21 20%	49 16%
Total	51 17%	53 18%	91 30%	104 35%	299 100%

Given the rampant statements about the relative boon to
faculty of color and the paucity of the job market for
whites, these data suggest a rather even distribution of
access of those having a reasonable experience in a job
market that is otherwise quite difficult

Only twenty-seven people in the study (9 percent) could be placed
in Prototype 1 and thus could be characterized as having been actively
sought out by a number of institutions. Of the white men, 6 percent were in
this prototype. Four percent of the white women, 9 percent of the men of
color, and 14 percent of the women of color were also in Prototype 1. Thus,
of the 192 persons of color in the study, only 11 percent were included in
this category. We observed a number of cases where selected institutions
were trying to diversify their faculty through designated target positions and
would seek out and encourage individuals to apply or to interview. Even in
these cases, where candidates were being solicited and sought out, the solicitations in virtually every instance were from only two to three institutions.
Some institutions reappeared several times in the study as actively soliciting
applications. Given the job market, the condition of being sought after is a
highly desirable position, but it does not suggest that these twenty-seven individuals were picking their ideal or even preferred work locations.

Forty-eight people (16 percent) were included in Prototype 2, those
characterized as having a good experience on the job market. Here, the distribution among the four race and gender clusters was somewhat more
evenly distributed. The proportion of white men, white women, men of
color and women of color in this category respectively were 18 percent, 21
percent, 17 percent, and 12 percent. In this category, white men and women
were slightly overrepresented given their representation in the total sample.

Since Prototype 1 and Prototype 2 included those having the most
job options, the first two prototypes were collapsed to look at participation
by race and gender. Twenty-four percent of the white men, 27 percent of the
white women, 26 percent of the men of color, and 25 percent of the women
of color fell into one of these two groups. Two conclusions emerge from
these data. Given the rampant statements about the relative boon to faculty
of color and the paucity of the job market for whites, these data suggest a
rather even distribution of access of those having a reasonable experience in
a job market that is otherwise quite difficult. The second conclusion is that
the vast majority of participants are not included in these two prototypes regardless of race or gender.

Because only the Ford group includes scientists, and because so many scientists are in the prototype in which no faculty positions were sought, this table might underestimate the degree of success of persons of color in proportion to the whole group, though this would be true only if scientists were sought out in the same proportion as others. To look at the data from this view, the same two categories were grouped together and examined while eliminating Prototype 8 from consideration. The percentages in this case were 24 percent white men, 31 percent white women, 32 percent men of color, and 31 percent women of color. Slightly fewer white men were represented in these two prototypes when the sciences are removed.

The distribution across Prototype 4 is fairly even, although it dips for white women, while Prototype 5 reflects more white men and women with single offers. If Prototype 8 is removed once again, one sees the differences shrink somewhat. The combined distribution for Prototypes 4 and 5 is 45 percent, 42 percent, 31 percent, and 27 percent respectively.

Prototype 6 includes those who sought faculty positions and found only substitute positions that did not fully utilize their talents and degrees. Thirty-three people (11 percent) were placed in this prototype. Twenty percent of the white men, 8 percent of the white women, 5 percent of the men of color, and 14 percent of the women of color were "underutilized."

Since Prototypes 6 and 7 include those who had found only temporary positions or who did not have faculty positions after applying for them, a combined description seemed to be in order. Here, the breakdown was 22 percent of the white men, 10 percent of the white women, 17 percent of the ethnic men, and 20 percent of the ethnic women. White women were the least represented group here, and white men most represented, but only by a negligible amount. These numbers reflect the job market, the use of postdoctoral positions in the sciences when faculty positions cannot be found, and also the limits that are set by some candidates in their search process. For example, one of the white men in the study who has a postdoctoral fellowship limited his search to New York City and, even further, to private schools because he didn't want to work at a state school. He applied for four positions and was not hired for any.

Looking at these two prototypes with Prototype 8 removed reveals a significant finding. The distribution across the four groups in this case is 22 percent, 11 percent, 20 percent, and 24 percent. Once again, the distribution is fairly even, except for white women, who were lower.

The diversity of experiences within groups was even more clearly reflected in Table 15, where racial/ethnic gender groupings are broken down. For example, although the study included a small number of Asian Ameri-

Table 15. Distribution among Prototypes by Racial and Gender Grouping

Proto-type	African American		Asian American/ Pacific Islander		White		Native American	
	Male	Female	Male	Female	Male	Female	Male	Female
1	4 13%	9 20%		1 14%	3 6%	2 4%	1 25%	1 20%
2	9 28%	6 13%			9 18%	11 21%	1 25%	1 20%
3	4 13%	6 13%		1 14%	4 8%	8 15%		1 20%
4	6 19%	2 4%	1 25%		6 12%	3 6%		1 20%
5	3 9%	7 15%	1 25%	1 14%	16 31%	16 30%	1 25%	
6		4 9%	1 25%	2 29%	10 20%	4 8%		
7	1 3%	5 11%	1 25%		1 2%	1 2%		
8	5 16%	7 15%		2 29%	2 4%	8 15%	1 25%	1 20%
Col. Total	32 11%	46 15%	4 1%	7 2%	51 17%	53 18%	4 1%	5 2%

can males, none were placed in any of the first three prototypes. A greater percentage of African Americans and American Indians were placed in Prototype 1 than the other race/ethnic groups. In contrast, while six Latinos/as fall into Prototype 1 (6 percent), fourteen (13 percent) were in Prototype 5, the grouping with a single job offer. There were also differences among Latinos. For example, while 9 percent of the Chicanos (Mexican Americans) were in Prototype 1, only 3 percent of the Puerto Ricans were so classified.

Proto-type	Mexican American		Puerto Rican		Other Latino/a		Row Total
	Male	Female	Male	Female	Male	Female	
1	3 9%	2 9%		1 5%			27 9%
2	5 15%	2 9%	1 6%	2 11%		1 33%	48 16%
3	3 9%	4 17%	5 28%	1 5%		1 33%	38 13%
4		2 9%	1 6%	5 26%			27 9%
5	6 18%	3 13%	3 17%	1 5%	1 100%		59 20%
6	2 6%	3 13%	2 11%	4 21%		1 33%	33 11%
7	7 21%	1 4%	1 6%				18 6%
8	7 21%	6 26%	5 28%	5 26%			49 16%
Col. Total	33 11%	23 8%	18 6%	19 6%	1 0%	3 1%	299 100%

"We are so few, it's amazing that most universities will say, 'We can't find anybody,' yet persons like myself are not recruited. I think I should be getting phone calls, and I don't get phone calls"

Of the nine American Indian participants, only two were placed in Prototype 1, although this represents 22 percent of the group.

Thus, when groups are disaggregated by ethnicity alone and by gender and ethnicity together, the broadly different experiences are highlighted. Indeed, an examination of these data suggests that white women, Puerto Ricans, and Asian American men were least represented in Prototype 1. While there are numbers of individuals who are reporting a good experience on the job market, the diversity of experiences between and within different racial, ethnic, and gender groupings is also apparent. Any declarations of a single bidding war paradigm are clearly not reflective of the experiences of many in the study.

Perhaps this quote from a Chicana in American and Chicano history captures most fully the experience about the myths of the bidding wars and being sought after:

> I would say that I find it a little surprising that I do not regularly get phone calls with regards to recruitment. We are so few, it's amazing that most universities will say, "We can't find anybody," yet persons like myself are not recruited. I think I should be getting phone calls, and I don't get phone calls.

6 Other Factors Influencing the Job Market Experience

THE JOB MARKET

With few exceptions, respondents in all fields described the academic labor market as "miserable," "lousy," and "rotten." A sociologist, for example, claimed that "At each interview I got, I was told that there were two hundred to three hundred applicants for this job. Some in places that were in the middle of nowhere. Even the lesser known state institutions," he emphasized, had "many, many, many applicants." A psychologist explained,

> There aren't a lot of academic positions. When I went into graduate school, the first thing everyone told us was, "Oh you guys are so lucky, this cohort is so lucky because by the time you all get your Ph.D., the job market will be really. . . in your favor because so many people will be retiring and all those positions will be opening up." However, the thing they didn't count on was the general recession we've fallen into, and as quickly as those positions opened up, they were closed because of financial constraints.

One of the Chicano scientists who ultimately took a position in industry (his only choice) after doing a massive search in academia and industry commented about the job market: "It was horrible. There was a large glut of people looking at the time. . . . There were a large number of Ph.D.'s coming out at that time, of high quality, in computer science."

An Asian American in comparative literature claimed, "While every year there are a number of attractive jobs, there aren't a huge number and because this has been true for so long, the competition to get jobs is re-

Overall, these new fields [dealing with race, class, and gender] are in greater demand than traditional fields, and faculty with expertise in these areas find more options

---

ally high. The job market is glutted with candidates who are finishing or have finished their Ph.D. and are hanging on in various part-time capacities." An African American woman psychologist commented: "There seemed to be positions, but in psychology the market is so crowded that there's a push now that either you have to have a postdoctoral experience, or if you are coming from a lesser university but you've been able to get publications, then you can go for bigger jobs." A white male in English stated:

> There are simply too many people and too few jobs. There were only three positions in my field this year. Each one of them received five hundred to six hundred applications. There are simply too many good people who I consider to be excellent scholars, people with book manuscripts under consideration or even accepted who don't even make the interview stage. . . . There are so many absolutely qualified candidates that universities are able to pick on the basis of what should be minor considerations, . . . not so much the caliber of mind, but questions of how many people on the faculty want someone who is young and hip and how many want someone who is young and not-so-hip. . . . There are academic fashions which simply go in and come out of style, some of which are significant, long-lasting changes within the profession, others which are quirks of fashion.

A Chicano molecular biologist, currently in a postdoctoral position, commented: "I would like a job in a university doing teaching and research. But within the last three to five years, the job market has been very bad. . . . I've started thinking of other options, like industry or getting an M.B.A."

NEW SCHOLARSHIP

There is a significant body of work being conducted across the country to transform the curriculum by integrating new scholarship dealing with issues of race, class, and gender. One might expect, therefore, that those faculty with expertise in these areas would find more academic job openings and would have more options for positions. On the other hand, many faculty of color and white women tell stories of being advised to stay away from such topics because they are often not seen as legitimate fields of study. This latter argument suggests that to be traditionally trained would position the candidate better in most academic disciplines.

The results from this study suggest that, overall, these new fields are in greater demand than traditional fields and that faculty with expertise in these areas find more options. For example, a Chicano in history commented that this was a "banner year" for history and, in particular, American history, because of the new scholarship in this area. However, even these conclusions must be treated with caution. Some fields, such as history and literature, appear to be infusing more of the new scholarship than other fields where such an approach might not be as well received. One Latino in psychology commented that "In my field there seems to be an emphasis on traditional research, which may affect minority candidates, who are more apt to do nontraditional kinds of research."

The study also suggests that faculty of color who have taken a more traditional route may not be at an advantage. For example, a Latino with a Ph.D. in economics who had left academe for an accounting firm felt he was not taken seriously for academic positions. An African American woman in developmental psychology and currently in a postdoctoral position got no academic offers. She said, "No one was beating down my doors." An African American male in medical anthropology found the job market somewhat better because he was in a traditional area with few minorities. "However, I was still not able to pick and choose positions as my [white] counterparts did."

White faculty whose primary field is ethnic studies were at a disadvantage in the study as campuses seemed to use those spots to diversify the faculty. One of the white men whose field is Chinese philosophy has had a difficult time finding a job. He perceives that programs advertising in this field are using the position to diversify the faculty. In addition, he notes that there are very few positions in this area at all.

Faculty of color in traditional fields, who should
be more desirable because of their "rarity," still
find it much more difficult to be taken seriously

Nevertheless, having expertise in the new scholarship while being
trained in one of the traditional disciplines appeared to be an advantage for
white men. Indeed, almost all the white men in the first two prototypes had
expertise in areas related to ethnicity. One participant, a white male whose
field is medieval history, applied for six positions and was seriously recruited
by all six institutions. When asked about the popularity of fields in history,
he commented that "minority history was a big deal . . . and my topic fell
into that in that I was studying minority history in the Middle Ages—specifically relations between Muslims, Jews, and Christians during that period.
Gender, ethnicity, and cross-cultural studies were also big, and if you had a
specialty in one of those areas you had a better chance of getting a job."

A white male who received a position in the classics said, "[His in-
stitution] should have hired a woman. At that time they had six men and no
women. I was a man who did feminist scholarship. It gave them an out. . . .
One more thing, . . . I didn't frighten the people."

Another white male with a Ph.D. in literature from a prestigious institution who has taken one-year positions commented, "I understand that
the growth market in American literature right now is ethnic literature because many departments do not have someone who has Ph.D.-level training
in that. On the other hand, poetry [my field] now is not of very much interest. . . . I think it will change eventually, but not now."

There is a certain idiosyncratic nature to the patterns, though, in
general, those faculty of color whose field was related to ethnicity were more
likely to have more choice than those who taught in traditional fields. Faculty of color in traditional fields, who should be more desirable because of
their "rarity," still find it much more difficult to be taken seriously. We also
sensed that those whose emphasis included issues of sexuality, particularly
gay and lesbian issues, might be at a disadvantage. Some of these differences
in experience may also be a function of specific fields. Perhaps in history
and literature there is more appreciation and awareness of the significance
of new scholarship, whereas in other fields there may not be.

While infusing new scholarship into the curriculum is an important
way to transform higher education and attract faculty of color, there is some

perception that some departments are merely trying to satisfy a need for diversity. Thus, hiring a scholar of color in a non-Western area fills several slots. We interviewed an African American woman who is an Americanist in English. She reported having a much better experience in positions related to African American literature than in her specialty, where her diversity was not valued.

Our results suggest that the experience of being one of the few persons of color in a traditional field does not necessarily place the person at an advantage, contrary to contemporary myths. At the same time, it appears that for white men in traditional fields, knowledge of the new scholarship is an advantage.

CHAMPIONS AND MENTORS

Participants in this survey were asked whether anyone had "championed" their search process. Championing activities were variously interpreted by respondents as active networking to locate good positions, personally recommending a student to a hiring department, lobbying to ensure that a candidate would be seriously considered, writing outstanding letters of recommendation, publishing with the student, or coaching the student through the various stages of the job search process. As an African American woman scientist noted:

> Yes, there was a person who went to the conference and told people about me. He also helped me set up the postdoc at [an Ivy League university]. And then there was another person on my thesis committee. . . . He gave me lots of advice, read my project descriptions and gave comments on them, . . . gave me ideas about places to apply, [and] told a few people, including [someone at] one of the places I got an interview, about me.

The extra effort put forward by established faculty members to help a young Ph.D. find an appropriate position is a significant psychological support in an otherwise highly stressful undertaking and is gratefully remembered by individuals, whether or not the job search process turned out as they had hoped

Another highly sought-after scholar offered:

> On the two campuses [where I applied] there was a person
> very instrumental in my application process and in making
> sure that I understood the process—helped me run through
> my talk and gave me pointers on the talk and the interviews.

Overall, 45 percent of the respondents in our sample said that they had experienced some form of championing (Table 16). A closer analysis of

Table 16. Degree to Which Factors Positively Influenced the Search			
	Known	Champion	Reputation
Yes	62% n=170	45% n=123	77% n=211
No	38% n=103	55% n=149	20% n=54
Don't Know	0%	0%	3% n=10

those who responded positively to the question indicated a striking relationship between those who had champions and those who had more success on the job market. Approximately two-thirds of the highly sought-after respondents (Prototype 1) and the "Good experience" participants (Prototype 2) reported having champions. More than half of the "Single but good choice" group" (Prototype 3) and the "Limited choice" group (Prototype 4) also reported having champions. But only about one-third or less of the respondents in Prototypes 5 ("Took what they could get"), 6 ("Underutilized"), 7 ("Not faculty, but applied for faculty positions"), and 8 ("Not faculty, never applied for faculty positions") identified any form of active advocacy during their job search. These results suggest that it matters a great deal to have an established member of the academic community promoting a young person's candidacy for a position. The role of champions in obtaining a faculty position is a subtlety widely acknowledged within the academic community but not frequently articulated. It is particularly important in obtaining the more coveted positions. One scholar presently employed in a temporary position said:

> In my job search I really did not have much support in this activity. . . . The only support from the faculty were in the form of letters of support. . . . No one networked for me. That is part of the reason I did not get the "high-status" jobs that were available.

The extra effort put forward by established faculty members to help a young Ph.D. find an appropriate position is a significant psychological support in an otherwise highly stressful undertaking and is gratefully remembered by individuals, whether or not the job search process turned out as they had hoped. One highly sought-after candidate acknowledged, "I had a lot of people pulling for me. I didn't read the letters of recommendation firsthand; I heard that they were just wonderful, 'that I could walk on water' kinds of letters." An applicant who was unsuccessful in securing a faculty position still said, "Everyone mentored me. I worked with wonderful people, . . . people who cared about me so much and who believed in me more than I did. They made me believe in me. They did everything and they still do. I am in touch with every single one of them and they are wonderful."

Surprisingly, the champions were by no means always the student's adviser, or even from the student's home institution. There were many examples of persons from the hiring institution who championed a person in the applicant pool. For example, a Chicano psychologist reported that the most important factor in his job search was that he knew someone at the school who championed his search. An American Indian woman teaching at a state college in the Midwest said that the chair of the search committee of the hiring school championed her job search. She reported, "He decided I looked like a good candidate and he supported my candidacy by phone calls and letters."

The Ford network of fellows worked extremely well for some young scholars. One Ford fellow commented, "The networking from the Ford meetings was also great. It was someone I met through Ford who convinced me to apply at [the institution where I now am]." Professional networks are widely utilized to identify those graduate students who will eventually be sought after, or who should be pursued once they apply. For two-thirds of our sample (including 85 percent of highly sought-after candidates in Prototype 1 and 74 percent of the classic academic individuals in Prototype 2), respondents were hired at institutions that had known them in some context, either as graduate students or as undergraduates, and where former teachers and/or colleagues could champion their application. Networking, therefore, emerged in this study as an important factor in the job search process. For faculty of color, other faculty of color were often critical to their success. Indeed, a Chicano historian now teaching in an ethnic studies department said: "The National Association of Chicano Studies, rather than a person, championed my search. I used my networks."

There is much written in the literature and in "how-to manuals" that emphasizes the important role of mentors. This study documents the significant role of champions in successful searches, but it also highlights that the source of champions is often not from graduate institutions but from professional associations and hiring institutions.

ADULT LIVES AND PREFERENCES

It is quite clear from this diverse group of respondents that visions of ideal institutional positions are not uniform. The notion that all faculty of color, for example, given their choice, would choose a prestigious research institution over other types of institutions is not necessarily true. For a variety of reasons, faculty preferences ranged broadly. In almost half of the cases, candidates severely limited their searches because of family considerations, cultural values and ideals, or geographic affinity. In such situations, ideal institutions were those that fit within the range of options available. Indeed, we noted preferences for every single region of the country. Moreover, participants ranged broadly in their preferences for institutional types. We heard preferences for liberal arts institutions, for diverse urban teaching institutions, for research institutions with doctoral programs, and for regional public universities. To assume homogeneity in these preferences is clearly not appropriate.

Furthermore, to assume that faculty today are able and willing to relocate anywhere is also false. Between the struggles of two-career partnerships and the desire to establish connections where one lives, many of our respondents could not and would not move. This situation creates regionally based resources that institutions could take quite seriously as long as there is no bias against someone who is more local. One of our participants commented, "I think the model of the old-fashioned academic who would do anything and go anywhere to live the life of the mind is not so."

Nevertheless, the bias against "local candidates" can be real. A white woman who just received a tenure-track position at her husband's institution explained her success in these terms:

> I went on the job market and accepted a job that was three thousand miles away from my family and made it clear to the community that I was willing to do that. . . . It gave [my husband's institution] a clear message that the academic community accepted me and gave me a job independent of my husband. . . . You have to be willing to take a job and establish yourself individually first. . . . Until I had a job and a grant they didn't take me seriously.

Others moved primarily to find two positions within geographic proximity for themselves and a partner. A heavily recruited Latina left a prestigious university only because another institution offered a position to her significant other. She said, "I would have stayed at [the prestigious university] where I already had a job. But they were unable and unreceptive to-

The comments individuals made about their commitment to their families yielded a large number of poignant stories and are cause for serious consideration by institutions of higher education

ward working something out." A white male who was heavily recruited for a position commented that he "entered the job market a second time when my wife finished her doctorate and we both started looking for academic positions. I was offered a job at [a prestigious university] and to keep me here [my current university] created an academic position for my wife."

The comments individuals made about their commitment to their families yielded a large number of poignant stories and are cause for serious consideration by institutions of higher education. Indeed, family considerations were responsible for some people choosing not to apply for faculty positions. They influenced which positions some people applied for, and they influenced how some individuals perceived their prospects for future success within academia. For example, a white woman in education felt geographically limited because of her husband's job. In lieu of obtaining a faculty position, she has put together three different postdoctoral positions. She states, "If I was willing to go anywhere and didn't have a relationship, it would be relatively easy to get a job. But because I am limiting myself geographically and because I am not willing to be separated from my husband . . . then you get into issues." She adds, "I always felt that I had to be flexible because of the way I set my priorities. . . . A faculty position would have been nice, but I was also willing to do other things." Similarly, a Puerto Rican woman scientist limited her academic search to a forty-mile radius from her home because of family considerations. She took a lab technician position for which she is very overqualified. She even applied for community college positions in her region, but was unsuccessful. Her husband is being relocated to a new city where she plans to try to find an academic position or at least a suitable postdoctoral position.

Other individuals have been able to find academic positions despite family constraints. A Puerto Rican woman psychologist who is married to an academic purposefully applied for jobs with her husband. They received several offers that allowed them to stay together. According to her, "The hardest part is . . . the two-body problem. It is really hard for my husband and me to be able to be at the same place. I think universities need to rethink how they deal with this." Similarly, a white man in the humanities who works part-time at his wife's institution expressed his frustration in these terms:

> The fact about academia today is that there are more and more couples . . . who need to live near each other, and the job market has to start respecting that and working with that more closely, whether it's through job-sharing, better and more secure part-time positions, or more spousal hiring policies that actually work. . . . Living apart and commuting relationships just don't work.

Many of the individuals in this study talked about the difficulties of balancing academic life with the demands and limitations of families. A Puerto Rican woman explained, "Now that I have a child, I can tell you that any research program that I may have in the future probably will not be at a major research university, because I am unwilling to spend the amount of time required to sustain the required research program." Similarly, a Chicana explained that obtaining a faculty position would be difficult: "It is difficult now because my husband is also a scientist and we have a brand new baby. The hours are hard and long and a two-career family is difficult." A white anthropologist who is a single mother added, "It is impossible to fit having and raising small children with a traditional faculty career path unless you have a wife. Most women out there do not have someone to serve the function of a wife." A Chicano in history who was quite successful on the job market commented that because of family responsibilities, he had a difficult time getting everything done. "The family responsibilities just kept me focused on certain kinds of options, and luckily I had good options, very good options compared to almost everybody I know in similar situations."

These results suggest both a challenge and an opportunity for higher education. The challenge will be the increasing difficulties of accommodating multiple family needs when national searches are conducted, unless institutions are prepared to build these considerations into search processes. The opportunity is that family considerations encourage faculty to develop

"There was active professionalization from the moment that you get there. They're preparing you to get published immediately, and they're preparing you to apply for grants immediately"

deeper connections, perhaps move less, and also to seek opportunities at a wide variety of institutions and regions of the country.

PREPARATION AND THE ROLE OF GRADUATE EDUCATION

We asked participants about what seemed to help and hinder them in their searches. In addition to the comments about self-limiting factors, publishing, teaching, and the job market, many commented on the role of their graduate institutions in preparing them for the job market. Participants commented about assistance in getting known, being championed, being introduced to the conditions in the market, and being prepared to interview and negotiate. Overall, 62 percent felt that they had opportunities to make themselves known, 45 percent commented that they had been championed, and 77 percent believed that they were helped by the reputation of their graduate institution (Table 16). It is clear that some programs do a much better job of mentoring students in this part of the graduate process. We heard many stories of students being encouraged to publish, receiving incentives and assistance in attending conferences, being introduced to other professionals, and being informed about strategies for dealing with a difficult market. In these descriptions, participants stressed the role not only of individual faculty advisers/mentors but also the general approach of the department.

One graduate of a prestigious program reported as essential and helpful that his institution "has a very good program. They actually run you through mock interviews and give you advice about organizing your packet." Another commented that at her institution "there was active professionalization from the moment that you get there. They're preparing you to get published immediately, and they're preparing you to apply for grants immediately. . . . I assumed that everyone did that until I went around. I never realized how unusual that was."

In contrast, other programs simply seemed to take no interest in making these efforts except for the occasional student mentored by a particular faculty member. Fully one-third of the participants did not have opportunities to make themselves known in professional circles.

A product of an Ivy League institution says, "Everybody gets caught up in the glory of the life of the mind and all of this, but I think that it's important . . . to give students an idea of what happens in the whole search process."

Some scholars undertaking postdoctoral fellowships are using this time to do the job search preparation that others do during the doctoral program. Given the number of instances in which faculty positions emerged through contacts made at conferences and other networking opportunities, not being encouraged in these areas can be a major impediment to success on the job market.

Given the reality of the job market, some candidates urged that students seriously look at nonacademic careers or at faculty positions at less prestigious institutions. Unfortunately, most were discouraged from considering other options and received no assistance in doing so. An African American molecular biologist, anticipating not being able to find a faculty position, said:

> I am trying to be optimistic about my future. You get into this mind set that you are doing what you love to do. But the mind set is that if you don't make it, you are a failure. . . . But I don't think I am a failure. . . . For Ph.D. training you become superspecialized, and for people who have good scientific training there are lots of jobs people could do. . . . The other problem is the negative stigma associated with not being a bench scientist or a researcher or a professor.

Our results suggest not only that graduate programs must develop both systemic and individualized opportunities for students to prepare for job searches, but also that consideration must be given to valid career options in a limited and limiting job market.

A number of faculty commented that they had
been hired because senior administrators were
forceful in getting search committees to diversify

THE SEARCH PROCESS

By and large, the faculty with the most choice, no matter what their background, tend to obtain their positions by rather traditional means. They have attended prestigious graduate institutions, worked hard, delivered papers at conferences, published, and struggled to get known. The presence and use of networks were obviously powerful strategies for these scholars. Many have had teaching experiences, though (to their regret) they found teaching to be less critical to search committees than publishing. Many have had to spread their net wide and settle for what they could get. Few have had the experience of being sought after, though clearly some have. Those with limited mobility or those who were more selective in their search found connections, past acquaintances, and prior institutional affiliations to be central. Over and over again, we heard stories of the importance of the networks created by the fellowship programs. The Ford Foundation's annual conferences have created powerful opportunities for scholars to network and for more senior professionals to champion the job search of younger ones. Indeed, where faculty are being sought it is often because of these fellowship networks rather than institutional practices.

Institutional hiring practices tend to follow similar and rather standard patterns. While many scholars of color received form letters expressing interest in them, most perceived these letters as merely satisfying affirmative action requirements—rather than as a reflection of institutional efforts to find and solicit their application because of what contributions they would bring to the institution. We heard about a few institutions that had clearly done their homework about promising candidates and made solicitations that were taken seriously. In most cases, the institution knew about the person's area of expertise, believed that the person would add strength to the program and approached the scholar on that basis. A number of faculty commented that they had been hired because senior administrators were forceful in getting search committees to diversify. They perceived that they had gotten the position as a result of Target of Opportunity positions and forceful leadership. Nevertheless, this strategy is controversial in terms of long-term impact (something that we were not able to study).

Given the tight job market, institutions can afford to be quite choosy in selecting candidates. In the culture of academe this tends to privilege individuals who have attended prestigious institutions, who have published the most, and who have, in the case of the sciences, had numerous postdoctoral experiences to their credit. It appears that except for cases in which ethnic fields are desired, these hiring criteria and specialization have grown in academic searches—no doubt eliminating many desirable faculty who otherwise would serve the institution well.

Many commented on what the "ratcheting up" of the value on research and publishing might do to a concern for teaching. A Chicano molecular biologist commented, "The publish-or-perish 'myth' is not a myth. . . . You should not have to be a publishing machine. So much emphasis is placed on your ability to get grants, and the ability to get grants is based on how much you publish, and the human side is lost.

"People are snobs. It's really awful. For a position we will get five hundred applications and if you are from one of the top granting institutions you have a much better chance."

According to a white male in medieval literature:

The pretense of doing searches adequately and fairly strikes me almost as pointless, because, in fact, it isn't as if there is one best candidate out of a whole lot of jobs. That is, if the system were working well, if there were say sixty jobs and eighty applicants, then in fact, the sorting process makes sense. The academic world in general has given itself over into a star kind of mentality. . . . Schools are looking for the person who is the hottest, boldest, fastest, coolest. . . . And I would say that, in fact, the needs of most institutions are not for stars. Everyone tries to be a star because it's the only way you can get a job. So that [everyone] is aping a model of success which is basically inappropriate. . . . To survive,

everyone has to pretend that they are all doing ground-
breaking work.

Moreover, in this study, there was an undercurrent of perceptions
that institutions were often threatened by persons who added truly different
perspectives to academe, to their fields, and to the values inherent in academe. One of our most sought-after participants commented that she
thought she was recruited because she was older and was seen as being
"safer."

An African American woman in sociology commented, "Unfortu-
nately, a lot of colleges aren't willing to look for a broad range of people. . . .
They are looking for very specific black people. . . .They are afraid of taking
people that are not from the most prestigious institutions."

A Chicano scientist commented: "The thing they care about is the
number of publications. They want your reputation. But if you are studying
a nontraditional thing, then it is difficult to get published. They are after
academics who study the subjects who are usually white. They like to see
their dispassionate approach replicated and they don't want you to experience your work emotionally."

There are clearly issues even for those who are sought after. A Chicana who had some choice of positions comments:

> Basically, institutions want to recruit faculty of color but they
> are approaching the recruitment in fundamentally the same
> way they always have without examining their structures and
> assumptions. They haven't said: "Perhaps we need to rethink
> the institution." They maintain the same norms and assump-
> tions. They do make efforts to bring faculty, but for many fac-
> ulty, institutions wind up being revolving doors, not only be-
> cause you get recruited by other institutions because the
> numbers are still so small, but because of issues. It is a battle-
> field. You are constantly struggling. . . . When you are fight-

ing every day for your sanity and survival, not around your scholarship, then your struggle is much different.

An African American male said, "There are undoubtedly good people in the academy interested in having diverse faculties, but they themselves are in the minority. It is still a very hostile place for minority people."

Recall the white male who received a position in the classics who said, "[The institution] should have hired a woman. At that time, they had six men and no women. I was a man who did feminist scholarship. It gave them an out. . . . One more thing, . . . I didn't frighten the people."

There were also numerous comments about the inhumane quality of the job market. One of our participants lamented the insensitivity of many hiring institutions:

> I wish that more institutions and more departments that were hiring faculty took the time to think about the candidate's experience. I experienced some that do . . . and others that really didn't and were insensitive in all kinds of ways. Many of them probably didn't even realize the ways they were being insensitive, not responding to applications or not responding for months and months, . . . not letting people know where they stand.

A white male in English explained:

> I've had an especially bad experience, but everybody's hurting, and people who are by any reasonable definition just brilliant are working part-time positions and non-tenure-track positions. People with families and three kids and can't find gainful employment. . . . If you are good you should get a good job. . . . If you're doing new work, interesting work, or maybe calling into question some of the ways that people used to think, you could just be blocked

It is also true that funding agencies, like employers, consider a candidate's credentials every bit as seriously as his or her performance and productivity, and that students at little-known schools have an inherent disadvantage in most selection processes, regardless of their abilities

out forever. There's a human cost in terms of people looking for jobs and suffering because they can't get them.

Because they are unduly competitive, seek more of the same, and are often quite political, search processes leave many young scholars with a bad impression of academe and its values. Not only is the process often seen as ineffective in attracting a diverse faculty, but also it is often seen as insincere—or at worst hypocritical. Moreover, the current dearth of positions allows institutions to ratchet up criteria which, in fact, may be harmful to institutional needs and values.

ELITISM

Embedded in the previous section on searches is a deep concern about elitism. Within academe, it is no secret that pedigree counts. Note, for example, that the overwhelming majority (93 percent) of the winners of doctoral and postdoctoral fellowships studied in this project received their doctoral degrees from top-rated Research I institutions. Fully one-third of the sample had received their doctoral degrees from Ivy League schools. Sixty percent of the group had received their bachelor's degrees from Research I institutions, but only 3.7 percent percent (ten individuals) had received their bachelor's degrees from an HBCU and another 3.7 percent (ten individuals) had received their undergraduate degrees from a women's college. It is true that top institutions train a great many gifted individuals. It is also true that funding agencies, like employers, consider a candidate's credentials every bit as seriously as his or her performance and productivity, and that students at little-known schools have an inherent disadvantage in most selection processes, regardless of their abilities.

Those graduate students who earn their degrees at more prestigious institutions, or with famous mentors, are generally perceived to have an edge in the academic labor market. As one young faculty member who had limited choice of jobs noted, "The market seems to favor people who are at elite or perceived-to-be-elite programs." The respondents in this study, most

of whom did earn their undergraduate and graduate degrees at highly prestigious institutions, and 70 percent of whom felt that the reputation of their
doctoral institution was a helpful factor in their job search efforts, frequently
spoke about the elitist attitude of hiring institutions. One part-time instructor offered the following comments on the matter:

> There's a lot of emphasis on where you got your degree,
> who you did work with. . . . I think there is a kind of screen-
> ing that goes on when people do these searches where they
> just basically throw out people from certain schools, just
> because . . . those schools don't seem to have as high a
> stature, . . . but I think it is unfair.

The process used to evaluate job applicants is less than subtle on
this point. As one young faculty member noted:

> For a position we will get five hundred applications . . . and
> if you are from one of the top graduate granting institutions
> you have a much better chance of surfacing in the top fifty.
> Usually these are very good students, but there are also good
> dissertations from really good students at "no name" institu-
> tions, but they don't get as much attention. I think it is very
> disturbing.

Having the "right" background extends beyond the doctoral study.
Science postdoctoral fellows know it is critically important to their future
success to work with a well-known mentor or in a famous laboratory. Knowl-
edgeable job candidates also realize that first positions can be pivotal in a
career. If one accepts a job at a university that is not known for research,
then it is very difficult to switch into a major research institution later in
one's career. In the words of one savvy postdoctoral fellow:

"For women and minorities who may have had a more difficult path than I had, the programs that they are in may not be the best sign of their personal quality"

> The way I see it you can kind of float in the hot places, in the higher-echelon places, and move laterally and make a career out of it. But if you step down to the second level, it is next to impossible to get back up. It's advantageous to float at the highest level as long as you can because it gives you the greatest job flexibility. . . . As long as I can stay in the major leagues, it will give me more flexibility down the line.

Elitism can work to the distinct disadvantage of women and candidates of color who may not have been as flexible or privileged in their academic path. Said a white male economist:

> There may be too much reliance on factors such as the reputation of the program you come from and the input of your adviser. For women and minorities who may have had a more difficult path than I had, the programs that they are in may not be the best sign of their personal quality.

FELLOWSHIPS

It is quite clear that without fellowship programs such as these, pursuing academic careers would be far less desirable than it is now. Overall, the participants in our study are surviving current conditions. In part this is a result of the fellowships they received and the direct and indirect benefits of being a recipient. The participants in our interviews were quite appreciative of the support from the three fellowship programs represented in the study. Financial assistance was extraordinarily important in facilitating completion of the programs involved and in limiting the need to work as much outside of the program. For postdoctoral fellowships, participants had much greater flexibility in options for laboratories and universities when they brought funding with them. One Ford fellow said:

The Ford Foundation was the best thing that happened to
me. . . . I think I've never had an opportunity to really express that. It allowed me to go to graduate school when I
could not have afforded it.

She also reported that it allowed her to pick the program and scholar she
wanted to work with.

A Mellon fellow agreed, saying, "The Mellon fellowship helped me
get my work done and made it possible for me to finish." Another commented: "Extremely helpful; I don't think people looked at my application
and said: 'Oh, she got a Mellon, let's interview her.' I think the real payoff
was that it gave me three years when I was able to write and further my
studies and it gave me more time than many other students."

One Ford fellow commented on the great job the Ford Foundation
is doing, citing its long-term commitment to the development of African
American scholars, Latino scholars, and American Indian scholars. He commented, "But there's even more Ford can do. A lot of minority scholars are
having trouble finding funding for research." He thinks because of the conservative mood in the country they are going to be having even more trouble
finding money.

A Spencer fellow commented on what it meant "as a graduate student to have an independent group say this is a valuable piece of research.
[It] gave me a lot of confidence in myself as a researcher and made me proud
of what I was doing."

A Ford dissertation grant recipient said that the fellowship allowed
her to devote more time to her research and looked good to other funding
agencies and academic departments. A Spencer recipient said:

I am not sure how well known the fellowship is, so I am not
sure the name itself made a difference. But having that support from Spencer in the year I was job hunting was probably far more important to me than name recognition. Psychologically, too, I knew that I was being supported during

the last phase of the work and that people were interested in what I was doing.

Many also felt that having received the recognition of these prestigious programs could only be helpful in searches and other selection processes. A white male said:

> I understand that [my institution] pointed to these features in my resume in making a case for hiring me, after they had decided on other grounds. I corresponded with the director of the Mellon four or five times, and he just had a perspective and panoptic vision that was very helpful when graduate school was seeming to take too long and it didn't seem to be getting any better. It was wonderful to have someone of his stature let you know that it was okay and that eventually we were going to get jobs.

The impact of programs is felt long after the financial support for those programs that encourage continuing networking. The fellowship programs differ in the degree to which they provide active networks for recipients. The Mellon Foundation no longer provides opportunities for recipients to meet. Spencer creates opportunities for current fellows to meet three times during the year. In addition, the American Educational Research Association's annual meeting is the location for a reception for present and past Spencer fellows. The Ford Foundation's program is highly unusual in the continuing support and opportunities for networking provided all current and past recipients. Its annual conferences provide a strong base of support, networking, and preparation. These meetings incorporate career advice, substantive academic sharing, professional topics, and many opportunities for sharing and networking. Our research has revealed the degree to which past fellows create opportunities for newer fellows on the job market. One of the scientists, an African American woman who was just beginning a faculty position, commented that she went to a Ford conference where they "talked about job searches and strategies and it gave me emotional support. In general people were useful, although scientists knew more what I was talking about." One of our participants commented that the Ford conference is "the oasis of my professional career. I have been to six conferences and I will go back as many times as I can."

7 Scientists

During this research project, fifty-seven scientists were interviewed. While these individuals were assigned to at least three different prototypes for our overall analysis, the research team recognized that the situation in science is sufficiently different to justify analyzing the data from this group separately.

The sample of scientists in this project included twenty-seven men and thirty women between the ages of twenty-seven and forty-four, although most (80.7 percent) were between the ages of thirty and thirty-seven. They represented all the major scientific fields, including biology, chemistry, physics, engineering, geology, and geography. All were winners of Ford predoctoral or postdoctoral fellowships within the last five years. Since this fellowship is limited to members of minority groups, all were scientists of color. Of this group, nine (four men and five women) currently hold tenured or tenure-track academic positions, one man holds an academic position which is not tenure track, and sixteen (nine women and seven men) are employed in industry, including the management of clinical research facilities and academic programs. More than one-half (54 percent) of the group, thirteen women and eighteen men, hold postdoctoral research appointments, even though they finished their degrees up to six years ago.

The scientists are a unique group among the larger sample in this study, because for the vast majority, while the Ph.D. is the terminal degree, it is by no means considered sufficient credentialing to take up a professional position in a scientific field. Instead, one or two postdoctoral appointments are considered necessary prerequisites for professional employment. As one interviewee said, "The majority of us in the sciences know that postdocs and publishing results are very important in setting up job opportunities for the future, especially in research institutions." A molecular biologist

For scientists, then, graduate work is a kind of
apprenticeship, which leads to the intermediary
journeyman position of postdoctoral fellow

noted, "It is practically impossible to enter the job market directly after
graduating with the Ph.D. Postdoctoral experiences are necessary—at least
two—if you want to go into a faculty position in the future." The reasons for
the necessity of doing postdoctoral work are also widely agreed upon. As a
Puerto Rican biochemist explained, "Postdocs are important in our field because we learn new techniques that are useful in our research. The more research techniques that you have at your disposal, the more marketable you
are." New techniques are only part of what one gains from the postdoctoral
experience, however. A Chicano neuroscientist elaborated on other factors
less obvious to an outside observer:

> No one gets a job after their Ph.D. unless they want to
> teach in a community college or a third-rate state institu-
> tion. If you did, you wouldn't get funding for your lab. The
> National Science Foundation or some other funding agency
> wants to fund someone who has had some experience. They
> can't risk funding someone who hasn't done a certain amount
> of research and shown they know about managing a lab and
> producing results. When you finish your Ph.D., you are ex-
> pected to do a postdoc. Even then it is hard to find a job.
> They say you know a lot about this field, but you need to
> know something about another line of research, so you do a
> second postdoc and try again.

For scientists, then, graduate work is a kind of apprenticeship, which
leads to the intermediary journeyman position of postdoctoral fellow, where
the fresh Ph.D. can master a new set of technical abilities, obtain grantwriting
experience and proof of future "fundability," garner experience in laboratory
management, enhance her or his publication record, and make valuable connections for the future. Successful completion of both stages of training are
now considered mandatory for the attainment of scientific craftsman status.
The process for obtaining postdoctoral positions is not akin to the process for
being accepted into graduate school, where standardized test scores and aca-

demic performance in undergraduate school weigh heavily. Nor is it similar to the procedures used to hire faculty, where nationwide advertised searches are the norm and equal opportunity procedures are rigorously applied. Instead, the process for securing a postdoctoral appointment depends heavily on a person's networking resources, on whom your adviser knows or whom you have met at a scientific gathering. Many times graduate students in our study made arrangements for postdoctoral positions through talking informally to scientists at professional meetings. Another methodology was succinctly synopsized by a University of California–Berkeley postdoctoral student:

> When you are about a year-and-a-half away from graduating and you start thinking about postdocs, you simply start reading and asking your professors about people who are good in the area you are interested in. You just fly out to the school to visit the laboratory, talk to the people in the lab who work there—because the professor wants you to meet the other lab people, probably because they get a feel from those lab people about how good you are—then you talk to the professor one-on-one for a while about what you are interested in and what you might want to write a grant on. Then [sometimes] you have to give a seminar on your graduate work.

Although many postdoctoral positions are advertised in professional scientific journals every year, numerous others are arranged quite casually. Certain lab directors are known because of their concentrated areas of research, publications, and references. These laboratories receive many requests from graduate students, so they have a good choice in selecting students and never have to advertise. As an African American female virologist reports:

> It would be nice if all positions were advertised. . . . In fact, the majority are not advertised. . . . That's where the network comes in, that's where the pedigree comes in. Often . . . the

We did not find evidence that the scientists interviewed harbored much resentment for this extended training period. As one Latino applied physicist mentioned, "In many ways it is a wonderful opportunity to do research without any other requirements of regular faculty"

> positions that are advertised are the ones that are difficult to fill. . . . It's not uncommon to have someone get a postdoc where she currently is because she formerly was in a lab with someone else who had done a postdoc there years ago. It's all who you know, where you went, and who your thesis advisers know.

Finding a postdoctoral position is not considered to be difficult. As one interviewee put it,

> Finding a postdoc is very easy because we are cheap labor. Postdocs are already trained, most postdocs are responsible for generating their own grant money to pay themselves and you have to work hard. You are still in that cheap labor category that makes you desirable. From a principal investigator's perspective, if one of your postdocs is successful, it helps you.

There is competition, however, for placement in laboratories with strong reputations or high visibility. Throughout academe, pedigree counts. Graduating from prestigious schools and working with prominent figures is a distinctive advantage in initiating a successful career. Science is no exception, and most of our interviewees recognized this. One Chicano chemical engineer, now an assistant professor at a state school, noted, "There's a lot of emphasis on where you got your degree, who you did work with." An industrially employed geophysicist said, "It hinders you if you don't come out of the top three institutions in this field—CalTech, MIT, and Harvard. It is your adviser that is really important." An African American chemical engineer employed at an industrial research laboratory said, "It's important that people are made aware of how the reputation of the school or working with a prominent professor really makes a difference to getting a job." Since the postdoctoral fellowship is most commonly the position from which the novice scientist looks for a job, the importance of placement cannot be overlooked. Also, active mentorship at this stage can have a critical effect on a person's future career. As one biomedical physicist put it, "I wanted to find someone who would take a vested interest in my welfare and progress, not someone who would just give you a lab and a space and tell you to go away and do something." Said another, "In my field, where you did your postdoc is looked at more than where you earned your Ph.D. For employment in academia, the person you do your postdoc with is very important."

We did not find evidence that the scientists interviewed harbored much resentment for this extended training period. As one Latino applied physicist mentioned, "In many ways it is a wonderful opportunity to do research without any other requirements of regular faculty. There are very few distractions besides working in the laboratory." A Puerto Rican woman neuroscientist said, "[The postdoctoral experience] is giving me more liberty than I will ever have [again] to do what I want in the lab. So, I can enjoy the experience."

It must be kept in mind, however, that the training period for a successful scientific academic career is effectively double that for graduate students in other disciplines. During the postdoctoral period, the salary level (about eighteen thousand dollars) and working arrangements are only slightly better than those for graduate students. The prolonged investment in terms of time and the postponement of reasonable levels of remuneration is a hardship felt by all, but particularly by minority members, many of whom come from modest backgrounds. Recall the American Indian woman who now works in a privately funded medical research laboratory and who lamented the reality of the scientific marketplace by saying, "You spend five years getting a Ph.D. and then you do two to six years as . . . an apprentice [postdoctoral fellow] and then you go to a job market that would offer you less than what you could have gotten if you'd gotten a two-year M.B.A."

Such a situation might be conscionable if employment prospects were good at the end of the pipeline. But the market for scientists is no better, and may in some instances be substantially worse, than that for new Ph.D.'s in other disciplines. The postdoctoral position therefore serves not only as advanced training in a discipline, but also as a "holding tank" for

The scientific establishment in the United States, especially as represented in the major research laboratories, is not generally perceived to be aggressively engaged in issues of diversity

those highly skilled individuals who are not successful on the job market. A structure that nurtures an ever-increasing pool of highly qualified applicants and allows prospective academicians to keep pursuing research and improving their publication record inevitably increases the competition for those jobs that do become available. This state of affairs benefits individual laboratories and the scientific establishment as a whole. It is an effective method for maintaining a highly skilled workforce that makes critical contributions to the productivity of a laboratory group, thereby enhancing the reputation and the grant-getting abilities of the head scientists. It does so, however, at the expense of the younger scientists who are being groomed to take over positions that may not exist. This reality does not go unnoticed by postdoctoral fellows who find themselves in limbo. One Chicano astrophysicist, who spent four years as a postdoctoral fellow, could not find a faculty position despite an aggressive search. With his postdoctoral funding running out and a family to feed, he took a job in industry. This man observes:

> It is irresponsible to continue producing Ph.D.'s when there's no market for them. People train for five or six years to get a degree and there's no job for them. When you grow up in the academic culture, it can be a real shock when you find out there are no jobs [and] you could have been training all that time for something which is realistic. Applicants and entering students should be warned in advance that they have very little chance to do what they think they want to do. It is convenient for [the labs] to get cheap labor. . . . They have highly talented people they pay ten or twenty thousand dollars a year who bring in their own funding, so it is to their [the system's] advantage to continue producing Ph.D.'s.

The primary question of this research project is what roles gender and ethnicity play in the academic labor market. While 41.5 percent of the scientists interviewed acknowledged that gender and/or ethnicity had played some role in their own appointment as a faculty member, postdoctoral fellow in a research laboratory, or industrial scientist, 58.5 percent held a different view. Forty percent of the scientists in our sample felt gender and/or ethnicity had nothing to do with their appointments and 18.9 percent said they were unsure of what role, if any, gender and ethnicity had played. Similarly, only 42.6 percent of our interviewees said they saw some effort being made by universities to diversify their faculties. Fifty percent said that they saw no such effort or that the efforts were "all talk and no action." Another 7.4 percent were unsure whether or not the academic establishment was making sincere efforts towards diversification of faculty.

The scientific establishment in the United States, especially as represented in the major research laboratories, is not generally perceived to be aggressively engaged in issues of diversity. Frequently, people claim that social issues have little to do with science. A Chicano postdoctoral fellow explained, "Biology is a very international community, so nobody really [cares] about nationality, ethnicity, and gender." A Puerto Rican chemistry postdoctoral fellow at UC–Berkeley noted, "In this research team . . . we have people from Japan, Finland, etc. We are a diversified group. I was hired for my scientific background and expertise and not for my racial background." A Chicana biochemist in the same laboratory observed, "There's so few ethnic minorities in my field that, you know, it really doesn't play a role because it's not really an issue." A geophysical researcher in private industry felt, "The minority issue doesn't enter into it much at all." A woman postdoctoral fellow in biochemistry stated, "There is very clearly a bottom line that they want someone who will be productive, and they want someone who has money—that's what they look for—but they're not looking to diversify their laboratory in any way. I've never met any scientist who's looking to diversify his laboratory, even the real open-minded ones." As a Chicano plant geneticist put it, "It doesn't matter what color or nationality you are, all they want is the best, period. Regardless of what the publicity may say, [diversity] is just not a factor."

Although many of our respondents did not choose to differentiate ethnicity and gender as diversity factors in the marketplace, some were quite careful to draw attention to distinctions between them. An African Ameri-

One female African American postdoctoral fellow noted, "As a postdoc you are fairly protected. There is special money available for minorities. . . . More than wanting to diversify their ranks, I think institutions want the money that minorities bring"

---

can assistant professor presented evidence that white women were making more inroads into scientific departments than ethnic minorities. She said, "Look at any of these faculties—the top ten or twenty—and only a certain number of these will have a black person or a Hispanic person, but almost all will have a woman. I think they are trying harder to hire women. I don't feel an effort by departments to hire minorities." A Chicano physicist agreed with her assessment. He noted, "I find that gender is the most important determining issue in employment."

In securing a position at the postdoctoral level, it would seem that women and minority scientists have something of an advantage, not because of diversity initiatives supported by institutions but because of the fellowships provided by private foundations and government agencies available to support them during this phase of their training. There are many fellowships, including those of the Ford Foundation, the National Institutes of Health, and the National Science Foundation, that specifically support minority scientists to do postdoctoral work. A lab director is much more likely to accept a postdoctoral fellow who arrives with her or his own money than one he or she must support from his or her own grants. The fellowships are directly helpful to the individual as well, because the stipends they provide (approximately twenty-five thousand dollars) are 40 percent higher than the average stipends of a nonminority postdoctoral award. The fellowships often provide funds for research materials as well. A Chicano neuroscientist doing postdoctoral work in New York readily admitted, "My situation was a lot better than other people going into postdocs because I was starting at a much higher salary level [twenty-five thousand dollars versus seventeen thousand dollars]. Having my own money gave me a great deal more freedom than I would have had on someone else's salary line." There is, however, a certain amount of cynicism concerning the motivations of the laboratory directors in accepting postdoctoral fellows. One female African American postdoctoral fellow noted, "As a postdoc you are fairly protected. There is special money available for minorities. . . . More than wanting to diversify their ranks, I think institutions want the money that minorities bring."

Most of the members of our interview group of scientists of color felt that building more diverse faculties, in science as well as other disciplines, was imperative sociologically—for the good of the students in our evermore diverse institutions of higher education. A Chicana physiologist from a working-class background commented,

> They should take stronger actions when hiring minority professors. They do not know how important it is for students. I wish I would have had a female professor. Not to have them in the best schools is sad. We go to college. Many of us have had the worst teachers. We come from poor communities and do not have necessarily the most qualified teachers. We also do not have the resources. We are not always ready. If we see role models, then we would say there is hope for me. You can do it—*si, se puede*. I survived, but it would be easier if we had a helping hand. They should hire more minority women in the sciences.

Another Chicana physiologist, recently hired at a Southeastern public institution with only a few minority faculty focused on the effect of faculty of color on the undergraduate population.

> Where I am right now, the problem is that there is a perception of students who are minorities are somehow not as bright and capable of learning. . . . The faculty say, "Most of the minority students that I've had, most of the African American students that I've had, they're the ones who do worst in my class." . . . They don't even realize that they're pigeonholing, and that they're . . . setting up situations where these students aren't going to do as well. They don't realize that they may be treating them differently. I think that the faculty thinks of themselves as being not prejudiced, but the things that people say!

The number of minorities in science departments must be increased in order to make the working environment congenial for those who are there

---

Those who have been involved in mentoring relationships with other minority members emphasize its unique value, as does one Latina:

> The person that has been most helpful [to me] is Hispanic. He is well-known in his field. Many people have preconceived notions about what you can or cannot do and are not necessarily as supportive [to others] as they are to their own kind. These people may not be malicious but they can block your progress. It seems that when you deal with your own kind, you are more comfortable, more relaxed. It would be nice to have diversity in the faculty, to be able to mentor people like myself.

A Chicana physiologist remarked, "I have a lot of students who, once they found out that I am the minority adviser in my department, . . . they come in and try to ask me things. They're not comfortable coming to other people."

Although a few individuals addressed the fact that diversity in academe, including science fields, was important to broaden the perspectives of those driving research endeavors, this was not a major theme we encountered. However, many in the interview group articulated what majority faculty members do not readily acknowledge: that the number of minorities in science departments must be increased in order to make the working environment congenial for those who are there. It is clear from the comments collected in this study that at the present time many minority scientists do not feel they fit into the American scientific establishment. An African American scientist, who feels she gets along well with her colleagues, commented:

> Regarding racial prejudice in science, you should know that although people I work with are pretty open-minded and we have a lot in common (family, professional interests, politics, kids, etc.). . . . [But] as a black person you are never

over the hump. Caucasians always see you as a person of color when they talk about issues. You see it in their eyes, in their manner. You always have to be on guard. Although in many ways it is easy to stay on common ground, and really we have more similarities than differences, still a split can always develop.

Another African American postdoctoral fellow mentioned the discomfort he seemed to trigger in others at national meetings when he tried to discuss research with them. He noted:

Even when minorities enter the door, there is going to be a degree of cultural discomfort. I didn't anticipate that in science. The problem is not necessarily racism, but blacks and whites, especially the generation I work with, feel discomfort with one another. It's on my side and also on their side. The thing that bothers me about sciences is that I will have to work in this aura of discomfort the rest of my life. Most of the people I work with did not go to school with blacks and there was not integration in their day, and for many their first experience with minorities would be with people like me. . . . As a career, I'm wondering if I want to work in an uncomfortable environment. . . . I actually switched departments to chemistry, where there were mostly foreign students, and instantly I became at ease. Everybody there was essentially an outsider. That actually saved a large part of my graduate career. I think this cultural separation is the primary barrier to blacks and other minorities not getting Ph.D.'s. I think a lot of people don't want to admit it, but subconsciously I think that is the largest barrier. The inability to be just one of the guys in the crowd makes you so self-conscious that you are very uncomfortable.

"I think that as far as [the] postdoc goes, [ethnicity] has helped a great deal. I'm not sure that I like that. I would rather be hired on my own credentials." Minority scientists resent being treated as a demographic statistic rather than as a productive, active contributor to the advancement of knowledge

---

One highly successful Latino scientist in biomedical physics, who thinks he is the only member of his ethnicity in his research field world-wide, puts it this way:

> One of the main problems with my present position is that there are very few minorities in the department I am in. That has become an important issue in deciding where I want to go next. I haven't had any problem, but I prefer to have a much more diverse department in terms of students and faculty. . . . In terms of my work, I don't think the quality of the department is as important to me as the diversity issue. I want to work in a place where I am comfortable.

The "chilly" climate for women in science, already well-articulated in the literature, was echoed in this study. A good example is the experience of a Chicana postdoctoral fellow in biochemistry. She recounted the following story: "When I went to apply for the Ph.D. program, I was interviewed by one adviser. He said, 'You're married, you're a woman, you are not going to have time to work on a Ph.D. You can't make it in this program.' I really got angry with that comment." Since all of the women scientists interviewed were ethnic minorities, there was some disagreement over which factor contributed more to any problems they were facing. An African American postdoctoral fellow at a national research lab said, "Women are underrepresented, undermentored, and not taken seriously. I have noticed, however, that there is a hierarchy to prejudice. Once people can get over the fact that I am black, they hardly notice that I am a woman." An African American female chemical physicist ranked things differently. In her eyes, "Academia is a bastion of maleness, so I think being a female is more of a hindrance in academia than being black." An American Indian woman who works as a molecular biologist in industry agrees with this evaluation. She said, "I don't think women in science are taken as seriously as men. Even in my job place now, there are people in the administration that when they ask the doctors to do something, I'm not included. I think it is always there, the female part, rather than the ethnicity part."

Any inherent discomfort in a working environment is clearly exacerbated by the stigma that may be attached by majority members of a department to those minorities who have benefitted from minority- or gender-targeted postdoctoral fellowships, or from affirmative action or Target of Opportunity hires. One African American chemist, when writing grant proposals to support her postdoctoral work at a Northeastern institution, was advised by the principle scientist in the laboratory not to spend time applying to the "minority fellowship thing" because he felt she could win one of the other types and wouldn't "have to worry about what people think when they read [her] CV." A Puerto Rican biomedical physicist mentioned that a lot of his friends leave off the "minority" when they talked about their fellowships, because "When you say 'minority' fellowship, people sometimes think it is an automatic grant, that somehow you don't have to compete for it, as if it were an entitlement program and had no prestige. The scientific community, including most minority and women scientists, thinks of itself as a meritocracy."

The individuals interviewed in this study bristled when an institution seemed to value their minority status over their accomplishments. An African American postdoctoral fellow in molecular biology put it bluntly: "I think that as far as [the] postdoc goes, [ethnicity] has helped a great deal. I'm not sure that I like that. I would rather be hired on my own credentials." Minority scientists resent being treated as a demographic statistic rather than as a productive, active contributor to the advancement of knowledge. A Chicano physical chemist admitted, "I guess the thing that bothered me a lot was a sense that they were already trying to cater to my ethnicity rather than my scholarly accomplishments." An African American woman chemical engineer working at a national research laboratory stated:

> [Why] go to a university where people are going to be negative about your being there or think less of you because you're a minority or a woman. . . . They have to be at least

interested in somebody's research area and interested in her as somebody to fit in on the faculty. . . . The first thing that somebody says to me when they find out that I have a Ph.D. or that I'm interested in an academic position . . . doesn't have anything to do with my research area or my research ability. It's "Oh, you're black and female, you'd be great.". . . After you work really hard for years you want to say, "Yeah, but I did some research."

Despite the dismal outlook for employment opportunities, despite the less than optimal climate for women and ethnic minorities in science, and despite the ferocious competition for jobs, obtaining a tenured academic position was still almost a universal goal among the young scientists interviewed. Even though only 19.7 percent of the scientists in this study held any sort of academic position, half (48.2 percent) of them had applied for assistant professorships. Of the fifteen working in industry, ten had applied to academic positions but were unsuccessful in their job searches. Similarly, many of the postdoctoral fellows had also been thwarted on the academic job market and had chosen to continue doing research and establishing their publication record, albeit at very modest income levels, in order to enhance their chances in the future. A full 83.3 percent of the young scientists interviewed said that their primary goal for the future was to obtain a tenured professorship in academe. Only 9.3 percent indicated they were uninterested in university teaching and research as a profession, while 7.3 percent were unsure.

The job market in science is as discouraging as it is in many other fields. A big difference, however, is that when they enter the job market, scientists have trained two to six years longer than their colleagues, postponing professional remuneration and personal stability for future dreams that are becoming less and less attainable. As one Chicano postdoctoral fellow at a national research lab noted, "I would like to take a job in a university doing teaching and research, but within the last three to five years the job market [has become] very bad. There are no jobs for molecular biologists anywhere. Even the small universities and colleges will have two hundred to three hundred applicants, and the big universities may get over one thousand applicants per job."

The ever-lengthening pipeline of science provides some buffer to the dismal employment scene, but not indefinitely. As one perceptive biomedical researcher noted, "If you are six years out [after your Ph.D.] and don't have a job, you become damaged merchandise and no one will look at you." There is clear resentment heard in the comments of those who have engaged in trying to cross the bridge from postdoctoral fellow to assistant professor. A Chicano geophysicist commented:

> The one thing that frustrates me about the academic world
> is that they shouldn't train students in fields for which there
> are no jobs. Schools get grants and they need students, but
> the long-term prospect for jobs for those students is just not
> there. So you have a lot of frustrated scientists right now.
> There are no opportunities. What should be considered is
> whether students are trained in areas so that they will have
> a job in the future.

An African American biologist made a similar comment:

> Right now graduate schools are cramming people in one
> end and spitting them out the other end and [letting] them
> worry about themselves mentally. Right now, the way Ph.D.
> science is done—because more and more money is in fewer
> hands—there is a phenomenal need for people. The number
> of students going into the pipeline has just blossomed and
> there are no jobs for them when they graduate. Industry is
> no longer a haven either—they are laying people off. You
> have to be creative about what you can do with your degree.

There is a large literature documenting the underrepresentation of women and minorities in science in the United States. Major emphasis has been placed on getting and keeping representatives of these groups into the infamous academic pipeline. One might think, therefore, that those who have come to the end of the arduous training cycle would have an advantage in the academic job market. The experiences of our interviewees do not substantiate this hypothesis, nor in any way support the idea that minorities are taking jobs away from majority candidates. Of the eight scientists employed in tenure-track positions in this study, only one was hired into an affirmative action position. All but one (a historian of science) had postdoctoral experience, although two were hired first and allowed to have a year to pursue postdoctoral work before they took up their faculty responsibilities.

Some of our sample, approaching forty years old, decided to leave academe altogether, but not necessarily for higher pay. The scientists in this study who had left academe did so to begin to establish a career, to be treated with integrity, and to avoid the insensitive hiring processes they experienced in higher education. A Chicano geophysicist who went into industry did so after he was asked to apply to two academic positions—he felt that faculty members were being pressured by the administration to interview him and that they were not really interested. He commented that he hadn't felt like he had gotten a fair deal yet. Another Chicano geophysicist from a prestigious East Coast institution went into industry after applying for one hundred positions and receiving no offers. After this experience, his comments were acerbic:

> I thought that everything in academics was based on merit, including scientific argument, reputation, and so forth. From what I've seen, [as] compared to business, academics is much more politically driven—especially in terms of hires and funding. It's a much more competitive and dog-eat-dog world than I ever imagined.

An African American woman chemist who went to industry is not doing what she wants, but took the job after receiving only one undesirable academic offer. Worried he won't find an academic position, an African American male biologist is preparing for such alternative careers as patent law or curriculum development. He observed:

> We need to change how we train Ph.D. students. At least for Ph.D. training, you become superspecialized. . . . For people who have good scientific training there are lots of jobs that people could do, but you don't think of it because you have to be so focused on doing the research. We need people who are science writers, we need people who understand science to write text books and to design curriculum. You need to find a way to bridge that gap.

Many scientists in our study remain in postdoctoral positions, hoping that the job market will ease. A good example is a Chicano chemical engineer who studied at a Big Ten institution, and has thus far applied unsuccessfully for over thirty academic positions. Another is a female Pacific Islander who also applied for thirty positions. A chemist with an enviable postdoctoral position at a West Coast institution, she decided to continue her fellowship rather than accept the only offer she received—a two-year visiting appointment with no indication it could become tenure-track. An African American woman microbiologist doing postdoctoral work at a prestigious national research center poignantly articulated the frustration felt by many:

> My coworkers and I . . . are very discouraged. . . . There are so many other things I could have done, but I chose science because it was a challenge. I could have been an artist, musician, a linguist—because I was good at all those things, but I chose science because it was hard. Everyone who is in a postdoc here is depressed about the job market. . . . Nobody prepared us for this. We were all trained by extremely

There is a clear disjunction between the continuing
national efforts to increase the numbers of women and
minorities entering science fields and the opportunities
currently available to them when they complete their
education

---

successful people who do not understand what it is like now.
They didn't have to postdoc for so long. Grant money was
available. Now things are closing down. They could not
predict this. When we were in grammar school and high
school everyone was always saying, "There are not enough
scientists," but from the job market, that doesn't seem to be
true. The situation is herding us to the edge of the cliff.
There is nothing to do but jump.

There is a clear disjunction between the continuing national efforts
to increase the numbers of women and minorities entering science fields and
the opportunities currently available to them when they complete their education. The subjects in this study offered several suggestions on how to ameliorate this situation. A Puerto Rican pharmacologist suggested that individual fields have to take responsibility for controlling the number of graduate
students trained in their areas. He maintained, "Word should be out that some
fields are saturated, rather than encouraging people to continue to enter these
fields. There should be more realism, because after you have invested so
much time and effort in an area you almost have to stay within the field despite the bad market." One of the African American scientists in this study
suggested changing how Ph.D. students are trained, with reduced emphasis
on superspecialization and more attention paid to solid but broader scientific training that interfaces with other fields. It seems illogical to emphasize
highly specialized front-end research training for those who aspire to teach
undergraduates at schools that will not be financially able to equip laboratories with state-of-the-art equipment. With governmental funding agencies
facing severe cutbacks, fewer and fewer individuals will be able to support
their research endeavors from extra-institutional sources. Even for those who
do achieve a faculty position, the present system seems geared to training for
frustration. Many scientists in this study mentioned that there is a crying
need to be very honest with young graduate students about the realities of
the job market in various fields. As a Chicano computer scientist put it,

There is a need for people going into graduate school to get a full disclosure of what they're getting into. People going into graduate school can be naive about what the options are and what the realities are regarding funding, career paths, and so on. There is a need to keep the rhetoric in line with the reality. People say there aren't enough people going into the hard sciences, but that's not real. There are too many Ph.D.'s for the market.

A Chicana chemical engineer currently employed in industry suggested that private foundations might take up the challenge, not only of supporting the training of young women and minority scientists but of preparing them for what lies ahead. There is, of course, the underlying fear that with a scientific community not seriously committed to diversifying its membership, any cutbacks in the numbers of graduate students might inevitably mean a widespread reduction of women and minorities entering the fields in which they were never made to feel welcome. But this is exactly what must not happen, and where the greatest challenge for the future lies.

8 Messages to the World

DIVERSITY EFFORTS

In this study, underlying the stories and experiences of even those who have had the most success on the job market was a continuing sense of cynicism and ambivalence about commitments to diversity. Many felt that without continuing pressure, institutional efforts to achieve faculty diversity will decrease. Current efforts to diversify the curriculum and scholarship have created increasing areas of expertise for which faculty of color are more likely to be sought out. However, commitment to diversity and creating a campus that is supportive of diversity may or may not be reflected in these positions or in the processes used to fill them.

Many scholars, of all racial and ethnic backgrounds, perceived that institutional efforts to diversify were more talk than action (with some exceptions). As Table 17 reveals, three-quarters of the participants observed institutions saying that they wished to diversify. About one-third of our interviewees commented voluntarily that they thought this was "more talk

Table 17. Perceptions on Diversity: Institutional Action and "All Talk, No Action"		
	Institution Addressing Diversity	"All Talk, No Action"*
Yes	74% n=213	31% n=88
No	22% n=64	
Don't Know	4% n=10	*voluntary response

"White scholars are given the opportunity to fail, but minority scholars must never fail or they will be labeled unqualified"

than action." Even faculty who had a relatively good experience on the job market often remarked on the issue.

An African American woman in literature commented about the push at her institution to hire persons of color. Out of eleven faculty hires, there was one person of color. She said, "One of the main excuses is that black people will not want to come here. . . . I have been lucky personally, but the notion that it is easy to get a job if you are a person of color is not true."

Many institutions claim that they simply cannot find appropriate candidates of color to apply for their available openings, but the minority scholars interviewed in this study questioned such claims. Said one scholar who wound up with a limited choice of jobs, "Institutions say that they cannot find a qualified minority candidate, but you never hear that an institution can't find qualified white male or female candidates. The assumption is that if you are not black or Latino, then you are qualified. . . . White scholars are given the opportunity to fail, but minority scholars must never fail or they will be labeled unqualified."

One Chicano graduate of a prestigious institution left academic life commenting that he did not feel he was taken seriously for positions. He said, "I didn't see [diversity efforts]. . . . Not one institution seemed interested in my cultural background."

An African American woman in history commented about the need for change: "I think there's still this myth that if you're a person of color and, God forbid, a woman of color, then these doors just open up. I don't really see that. So often the environment can be hostile, if not indifferent." Several respondents agreed with her, noting that it is possible for women and minorities to "get in the door," but once inside the university structure, there is no support.

White males, who might have used diversity efforts as excuses for their own limited number of job offers, were as likely to criticize institutional efforts to diversify and to distrust the rhetoric. A white male economist reported, "The job market worked well for me. There may be too much reliance on factors such as the reputation of the program you come from and the reputation of your adviser. For women and minorities who may have had a more difficult path than I have, the programs that they are in may not be the best signal of their personal quality."

A white male art historian says that there is a "lot of talk about diversifying, but when push comes to shove there is still a lot of hiring of white males, and I'm a white male."

Similarly, a white woman in cultural studies said:

> By requiring particular positions to be minority positions
> there is a certain sense that other positions don't have to
> be . . . . Race and ethnicity are a mixed bag. There are a lot of
> people running around saying that minority candidates are
> getting all the jobs. When I look at who we hired, of the
> twelve jobs available we hired only one minority and we got
> special funding for her.

Another white male in classics said:

> A lot of people in my demographic group talk about "the
> lost white male syndrome" and say that all the jobs are
> going to women. I really don't think that's true. The field is
> still largely dominated by men and incredibly dominated by
> whites. . . . The inherent bias in the field is so strong that
> women candidates are just not taken as seriously from the
> interview stage onward.

A similar point of view was expressed by one of our African American participants who, like many others, had his degree from a prestigious institution in a technical area of the social sciences. He commented:

> When I graduated, I thought I would be highly recruited,
> but that was not true. My white classmates had a choice of
> opportunities. Universities invited me because they wanted

"But there's been some difference between situations in which [the effort is] simply there to make for a more diverse mix of human beings, versus really trying to fundamentally change the way we do scholarship and the way that the curriculum is instituted, scholarship is maintained, academic communities are built"

to pay lip service and also show in their affirmative action numbers that they interviewed a minority.

One faculty member, an African American male who received a finance degree from an Ivy League school and for purposes of this study was put into the second prototype because he received multiple job offers, commented that he did not "feel like a hot commodity." Indeed, he felt that the kinds of offers and places were not what he wanted. He commented about the diversity efforts on campus, "It's bull—you have deans sometimes saying some things, and you have the faculty who want no part of it. It is just not a priority to them."

Another African American female in the social sciences with degrees from prestigious institutions, publications, and teaching experience accepted her only offer and is happy at her institution. Still, she felt that her ethnicity hindered her. She noted, "Campuses lack the will. They might interview and recruit African American faculty. . . . But when [the field is] reduced to two people, the black is not hired. I observed this in six of the last hires at my institution."

One of our most sought-after candidates expressed the following sentiments about institutional commitments to diversity: "[It's] a lot of lip service and . . . window dressing." He reported that one place wanted to hire him to continue the tradition of having one African American scholar on campus. He, conversely, wanted a place where he could serve African American students and have colleagues like himself.

Another candidate who has flourished in his academic life commented about diversity:

I think in each of the places I have been, it has been a sincere effort. Most of these institutions have recognized that they are not diverse enough and have wanted to have faculty of color on board. But there's been some difference between situations in which [the effort is] simply there to make for a more diverse mix of human beings, versus really

trying to fundamentally change the way we do scholarship
and the way that the curriculum is instituted, scholarship is
maintained, academic communities are built.

Several respondents voiced concern about using "Band-Aid" strategies to deal with major wounds. As one highly successful minority faculty member phrased it,

> I would like . . . to find ways to have institutions address
> these [diversity] issues fundamentally and not just to . . .
> hire more faculty of color and put them into the same institutional structure that has not changed. That is not addressing on an institutional basis issues of racism, and sexism,
> homophobia, and class differences and what they mean. . . .
> Unless we begin to do that consciously, systematically, and
> openly as a community of scholars and people in institutions of higher education, I do not see too much change.

While most respondents were measured in their responses to our inquiries about their observations of institutional initiatives to increase faculty diversity, some were vehement in their denunciation of racism in the academy. Observed one such faculty member:

> The racism is incredible. It's rampant. I think people need to
> reexamine their own thoughts and feelings about people they
> are hiring, about affirmative action issues. . . . They tend to
> evaluate minority candidates on the same criteria used for
> European American candidates and we don't come from the
> same backgrounds. We can't be expected to look the same.
> They want to make us into little white people. We can't be
> and we shouldn't be. . . . When you are hired because you are
> a certain ethnicity, then people look at you as if you are important when you walk in the door and you spend a lot of

"The worst mistake would be to end affirmative action instead of strengthening it. It's not a question of political correctness, it's a question of survival"

time proving that you are too. . . . But even if you are competent, other faculty members always feel that you are not as competent as other people they could have had.

AFFIRMATIVE ACTION

It is clear from all of our interviews that affirmative action is supported with some ambivalence. People want to be hired for their scholarship, their abilities, and not solely for their ethnicity. Indeed, many faculty of color had little respect for or interest in those schools that sent out general mailings urging minorities or white women to apply. It was viewed by many as insulting and reflected little genuine interest in the candidates themselves. Some respondents spoke about their discomfort going to an interview not knowing whether they had been granted the interview because they were a minority and it was either "the right thing to do" or something that "had to be done," and feeling highly insecure about whether they were being taken seriously as a candidate. One African American scholar stated rather matter-of-factly, "I have the sense that people interview me always, even if they are not interested at all. I suspect that this is because they need to fill out the minority quota forms. . . . I think that minorities are the target for that all the time."

Despite a certain ambivalence among the majority of minority scholars in this study concerning affirmative action measures, there was deep concern about a retreat from affirmative action and strong support for it. One highly successful African American scholar spoke eloquently in defense of affirmative action:

I think if there have been programs which have had a major impact—not only in changing the colors of the university, but in changing the real nature of scholarship in the university—it has been the affirmative action programs. . . . I have an incredibly basic commitment to these programs and I would not be in academia without them. . . . I have been supported by these programs completely from the very time I left high school, and I know that I would not be here without these programs, so I take these assaults [on affirmative action] very personally. I feel that there needs to be more people, more institutions, more foundations which need to stand up very straight and say, "Look, we have transformed higher education for the better. We need to do more, not less."

Other respondents spoke plainly about their fear that the current backlash against affirmative action would reduce any institutional incentives to diversify and would work against future faculty of color. One scholar stated bluntly, "If we don't keep affirmative action, we won't see minority faculty in higher education."

Although ready to admit that affirmative action has not succeeded in resolving the problem of the inequitable participation of women and minorities in higher education, another scholar nonetheless felt, "The worst mistake would be to end affirmative action instead of strengthening it. It's not a question of political correctness, it's a question of survival. It's about the quality of life in this country. . . . To freeze us all out is asking for disaster."

A third remarked, "The door was never open and that is what is scary. If we go back twenty-five to thirty years and pretend everything is okay, we will be wrong. It will only aggravate political, social, and racial tensions. We need to accept who we are as Americans and not be afraid of each other. The politics we see tend to divide us."

MESSAGES TO THE ACADEMIC WORLD

As a part of this survey, the holders of predoctoral and postdoctoral fellowships were asked if there were any messages they would like to convey to the academy about their experience in the academic labor market and/or their experiences as graduate students, young faculty members, or professionals. The insightful and incisive comments offered in response to this open-ended inquiry clustered around four main topics:

1. Recommendations to downsize doctoral programs to bring them more in line with the needs of the academic labor market
2. Pleas to inform students early in their graduate career about the realities of doctoral-level employment in their field, along with suggestions that graduate students be given specific preparation in job search skills and in the management of the entire job search process in order to relieve the psychological stress many experienced
3. Reminders of the serious problems faced by couples and families attempting to coordinate professional and personal lives in academia
4. Calls for support for junior faculty members, particularly for women and faculty of color

DOWNSIZING DOCTORAL PROGRAMS

For those individuals who have had a difficult and/or disappointing experience in searching for a tenure-track position, the source of the problem seems straightforward—that is, that American colleges and universities are producing too many doctorates for the current job market. This observation was made over and over, particularly by young scholars in fields such as English, philosophy, religion, physics, and computer science, where a single opening will receive several hundred applications. In the words of one scholar, "People should be discouraged from going to graduate school. We are overproducing Ph.D.'s." Another offered, "I think there needs to be a scaling down of graduate programs across the country to match the low job market. It is cruel to produce people that aren't going to get jobs. Programs will have to be more responsible."

There is a growing cynicism among many that graduate faculty are slacking in their ethical standards, training large numbers of students in order to ensure their own jobs at the expense of the future well-being of these students. As one frustrated scientist stated,

> I think it is irresponsible to continue producing Ph.D.'s
> when there's no market for them. People train five or six
> years to get a degree and there's no job for them. . . . Appli-
> cants and entering students should be warned in advance
> that they have very little chance to do what they think they
> want to do. It is convenient for them [universities] to get
> cheap labor. I mean, here they have highly talented people
> they pay ten or twelve thousand dollars a year, who bring in
> their own funding, so it is to their advantage to continue
> producing Ph.D.'s.

Another scientist concurred with this opinion:

> They shouldn't train students in fields for which there are
> no jobs. Schools get grants and they need students, but the
> long-term prospect for jobs for these students is just not
> there. So you have a lot of frustrated scientists right now.
> There are no opportunities.

Part-time or temporarily employed faculty members, as well as those
not able to find employment in academia at all, are vociferous in their dis-
may over the current oversupply of Ph.D.'s in some fields. One part-time
English instructor put it in these words: "For departments to be expanding
the number of Ph.D. candidates that they bring in, for departments to be
starting up new Ph.D. programs when they used to have only master's [pro-
grams], [is] difficult to justify because there is no place for the students to go."

The blame for the untenable situation is sometimes placed on university administrators who hold on to the economic advantage of a large
supply of graduate students.

> So many universities depend on graduate students to teach
> as T.A.'s that it is a sort of self-perpetuating thing. They
> admit graduate students because they need inexpensive

Graduate school faculty members have an obligation to provide a "full disclosure" of the realities regarding funding, career paths, the current job market, and projections for employment in the field early in the graduate careers of their students

sources of teaching rather than [because] they want to take responsibility for them.

Some interviewees blamed undergraduate faculty, whose influence in encouraging students to pursue graduate training is pivotal.

Faculty are doing a disservice when they encourage students to go to graduate school. They are in a position to know what the market is like . . . and shouldn't encourage people to go into a field where they cannot live the kind of life that the undergraduate adviser is living.

Blame was placed by others on graduate faculty, who are perceived to have the real control over graduate student numbers. One white male applicant who had to content himself with one less-than-optimal job offer was bitter in his assessment:

There is the practice of sort of promiscuously accepting people into doctoral programs without giving them a clear and honest sense of what their chances are of getting a job. I think a lot of graduate programs and institutions exist more for the vanities of the departments and for ways the departments can get more money out of the institution rather than [for] training Ph.D.'s, so that in the end they sort of sucker these people in and there is no hope of them getting a job.

Those who have applied unsuccessfully for faculty jobs, especially in successive years, are becoming jaded. One such recent graduate said:

I think it is immoral to encourage people to get Ph.D.'s. . . . There are far too many people with the degree. My analogy

for being an academic today is like being in a traffic jam. In
a jam, it doesn't matter how fast your car goes.

PROVIDING FULL DISCLOSURE TO GRADUATE STUDENTS
AND SPECIFIC PREPARATION FOR THE JOB MARKET

In the present difficult job market, the majority of young academics
in this survey shared the opinion that—at the very least—graduate school
faculty members have an obligation to provide a "full disclosure" of the realities regarding funding, career paths, the current job market, and projections
for employment in the field early in the graduate careers of their students.
This way, these students have a realistic expectation of what may lie ahead.
One respondent who wound up with limited choices of jobs after a broad
search noted that becoming a faculty member at a college or university is
the best career there is, if you can get a job. "If you can't find a position, it is
awful." As he put it, "Graduate school does not prepare you for the hazards
of the job market." Another woman, who also wound up with limited
choices, described the job market in her field as "cutthroat and competitive." She felt that "people need to know; they need to prepare carefully."

Needing to know what lies ahead is particularly important to minority students, who often arrive in graduate school with minimal knowledge of
professional career paths in the university. One African American scholar
who has not yet succeeded in securing a faculty position lamented:

> With graduate students in general, but particularly with
> African American students, it is important that at graduate
> school mentors take an interest in your career and give you
> some good and sound advice about what you're going to
> find afterwards.

Managing a successful job search in academia can be a very intricate
process, yet it is more the exception than the rule that graduate departments
will have any kind of systematic approach to imparting the information

about the procedures involved, and rarer yet to find a school that takes the time to "coach" its students through the process. The dominant model seems to be one of "rugged individualism." Some people are lucky and find mentors or others who will help. Most use word-of-mouth information passed down from one cohort of students to another. Almost all of the participants in this survey, whether or not their job searches were successful, mentioned that they wished they had known more about the search process at the outset. One Japanese American woman synopsized the situation well:

> As a graduate student you don't have a big picture of what is out there. It would be nice to have the opportunity to learn how to write a vita. One of my friends helped me with everything. You don't learn those things from your adviser. Right now the knowledge is passed on from recent graduate to current graduate. There should be a more systematic way of learning it.

A Puerto Rican scholar of Hispanic literature succinctly stated the opinion shared by many:

> Departments should never abrogate their responsibilities in preparing students for the job market. They should teach people how to go about the interview process, how to prepare and present your dossier and your application materials, and all that you have to do to apply for a job. We did it through word of mouth and one professor in the French department helped us out. But the department itself cared not too much about orienting the students that way. Graduate faculty should be more active in preparing students to go on the job market.

A member of Prototype 7 (those who applied for faculty positions but were unsuccessful in their academic job search) suggested that a good project for a foundation to sponsor would be to compile a booklet for graduate students about how to apply for faculty positions.

The psychological stress involved in academic job searches was a factor noted by quite a few respondents, particularly those who have been on the market for several years. One woman in English described her job search as "probably one of the least pleasant things I've ever done." An African American sociologist who applied for positions in the traditional way still described his job search as "a learning experience—basically four months of hell. . . . The process is fraught with opportunities and pitfalls." The experience can be draining emotionally, according to a white female English professor who said, "It feels awful emotionally to be judged and it is a very difficult thing. . . . Even though I had a fairly pleasant experience on the job market, it is still really emotionally quite horrible. It was most agonizing when I didn't get offers and didn't know why." A white male historian who settled for the only job he could get stated, "The job search can be so dehumanizing. It is critically important that interviewers take seriously people who apply for their jobs and not just treat them poorly." A white political scientist with degrees from one of the most elite schools in the country said:

> I really didn't think the job market experience would be this awful. I often sit and wonder if I knew it would be this difficult whether I would have made the choice that I made in 1989. I like what I do a good deal and I think it is worth staying with, but good heavens, it is pretty awful in terms of going through the whole process. It is very demoralizing and very tiring.

Many had the feeling that search committees forgot the human element in their enthusiasm to find the "right" candidate, particularly in a milieu in which the supply of available talent is so abundant. Lateness in response, delayed notification of selection or rejection, indifferent treatment during interviews, or, in the case of minority applicants, tokenization during interviews, take their toll on candidates and may leave scars that linger. Recall what one temporary faculty member said:

> I've had an especially bad experience, but everybody's hurting and people who are by any reasonable definition just brilliant are working part-time positions and non-tenure-track positions. People with families and three kids can't find gainful employment. I'm a little disappointed because I think that maybe there's too much concern with making sure that institutions always have a steady supply of candidates for their openings, but not enough concern with the human concern of the Ph.D. people looking for jobs.

PERSONAL PROBLEMS INVOLVED IN FINDING A JOB IN ACADEMIA

A concern voiced repeatedly among young faculty members with academic partners was the extreme difficulty, in an unfavorable job market, of finding appropriate employment for both which would allow them to live together. As one highly sought-after minority woman commented, despite her own enviable experience, "It is really hard for my husband and I to be able to be at the same place. I think universities need to rethink how they deal with the academic couple." A white male in literature agreed:

> There are going to be some kinds of changes as spousal situations become more and more common—it's going to have to be routinized as part of the job search. It is basically impossible, without extreme luck, to have an academic couple wind up at the same university, let alone the same department. Something about the way that credentials are judged has to be weighed with the human need to make spousal employment more possible.

A white homosexual professor stated the problem clearly:

> Three years ago I knew three other couples who were com-
> muting between Boston and San Francisco. . . . I think that
> institutions in general are not aware of the loss they take in
> hiring somebody whose attention is elsewhere a good part of
> the week.

In this study, geographic location was the most important limiting
factor in searching for and/or accepting a position, and the issue frequently
revolved around the location of a spouse's employment. Part-time and temporary faculty frequently were in their less-than-enviable position because of
family considerations. As one such scholar stated:

> There are men and women who are connected, . . . who are
> both in academia and who need to live near each other, and
> the job market has to start respecting that and working with
> that more closely.

It is no secret to anyone that the demands of an academic career
conflict directly with modern lifestyles. One candidate from Prototype 3
who had a single but select choice of a position commented:

> As a whole, institutions require practitioners to be on the
> model of a married, European man with a spouse at home. It
> requires a spouse that is going to be home taking care of
> kids, running the home, and maybe even doing the research
> for you. Neither men nor women have that anymore.

Among young faculty members it is all too evident that the traditional academic career path puts an enormous strain on anyone trying to
start a family. As one discouraged woman who is now employed in a nonfaculty position commented:

Women and minority members often experienced a disproportionately difficult burden associated with excessive committee assignments and student counseling

---

> At the same time, you are trying to climb the career path and you are supposed to publish and do an intensive job search and move from one side of the country to the other in search of the right position that fits your career at that time. . . . It puts an enormous strain on anybody who is trying to start a family.

The situation seems to be particularly difficult for women who have families and are trying to complete their Ph.D.'s or get tenure. The problem is rarely systematically addressed at a university and, the report found, "Women have to kind of figure out on their own how to deal with it."

CALLS FOR SUPPORT FOR JUNIOR FACULTY MEMBERS, PARTICULARLY FOR WOMEN AND FACULTY OF COLOR

Many new faculty members interviewed in this project expressed a sense of amazement at how much was expected of them in their new role. While all seemed to feel the heavy burden of preparing new classes and trying to get a research program off the ground, women and minority members often experienced a disproportionately difficult burden associated with excessive committee assignments and student counseling. A female philosopher noted, "Women and ethnic minorities get ground into the ground by being put on so many committees by virtue of being a woman or minority. I was put on so many committees and was thesis adviser to so many people—and I was too naive to realize how much extra work was being expected of me."

It was noted again and again that the Ph.D. is a research degree and prepares the recipient to carry out research in a field, not necessarily to teach in that field. Although many students teach during their graduate careers in order to support themselves, fellowship winners are frequently exempted from this necessity, so their first years in the classroom are particularly challenging. As several respondents emphasized, getting a job in the academy is only the first step. Succeeding in the multiple responsibilities of that job over the first seven years in order to achieve tenure is a much more challenging proposition, and achieving tenure is the universal goal of those working in academe. Many respondents noted the need for help and support during these critical first years in the university. An African American male sociologist observed:

> It's important to give [new faculty members] the opportunity to get their feet under them. In the long term, the institution will get more out of them, both because they'll be better positioned to give more and because there's definitely a feeling of obligation and gratitude that comes from having this. A person may not realize how tired he is from doing his research and his dissertation until he moves on.

Some people felt that this support should come in the form of a reduced teaching load. Others mentioned the need for mentors from among established faculty. A Puerto Rican woman in Prototype 2 felt there should be more information available on junior faculty development and on the roles and expectations for junior faculty.

9 Conclusions and Implications

MYTHS AND REALITIES

This highly select group of fellowship recipients is, as would be expected, doing well. These scholars have been educated by the elite universities and have been, as one participant stated, "legitimated by the prestige of their doctoral institution." The vast majority, regardless of race or gender, are in regular faculty positions or in postdoctoral positions appropriate to their fields.

The purpose of this study, however, was to address a number of propositions—propositions that we will now label as myths—concerning the academic labor market for recent doctoral recipients.

Myth one. Because there are so few faculty of color in the pipeline, they are being sought out by numerous institutions that must compete against one another in the hiring process.

Reality. The supply and bidding arguments are grossly overstated. Even in this highly select group of doctoral recipients, the difficulties of the job market and the limited number of options are more often the pattern than not. While some individuals clearly do report having multiple offers, virtually none find bidding wars to be their experience.

As part of the study, eight prototypes were developed to describe a variety of experiences on the job market. The first prototype was developed to characterize those who were sought out. Only 11 percent of our scholars of color were characterized in this way, with a wide band of variation within groups. The remainder of ethnic minorities were distributed across the prototypes. Moreover, few of even this select group could be characterized as being in a position of having institutions bid for them. When a candidate

It was not uncommon for our participants
to express regret that they had not been
recruited by a regional institution with
which they had some affinity

---

could negotiate, it was at the more modest level of items such as courseloads and research support.

Indeed, while institutions continue to describe their inability to find or attract candidates, many candidates are sitting in positions over which they had little choice and, in the case of science, in "holding patterns" of developing even more technological specializations that may or may not be essential for the positions that they will eventually assume.

This quote from a Chicana in American history might serve as a reminder about this myth:

> I would say that I find it a little surprising that I do not regularly get phone calls with regards to recruitment. We are so few, it's amazing that most universities will say, "We can't find anybody," yet persons like myself are not recruited. I think I should be getting phone calls, and I don't get phone calls.

Theoretical frameworks that assume that supply and demand will predict an individual's experience were clearly not supported by the study. In particular, such frameworks would suggest that the fewer the number of persons in a field, the more in demand these individuals would be. The results of the study, while not precise, suggest that scholars who introduce ethnic studies expertise within a discipline are more in demand than those whose studies have been more traditionally defined. This may suggest that search committees are more likely to take candidates of color seriously when they have already moved to take the new scholarship seriously. Scholars of color who are working in traditional areas like math or science may indeed find themselves at a continuing disadvantage in the current competitive job market. This is tragic.

Myth two. This myth focuses especially on the supply and demand in the sciences for faculty of color. The scarcity of faculty of color in the sciences means that few are available and those that are available are in high demand.

Reality. It is not unusual for institutions to cite the lack of availability of persons of color in math and science as the reason for the lack of diversity in hiring in these areas. Indeed, it is common for institutions to cite the number of African American mathematicians who receive the Ph.D. each year as an explanation for the lack of success in hiring. While these numbers are certainly accurate, this study revealed another, quite different reality. The vast majority of scientists in this study, all of whom are persons of color, continue to pursue postdoctoral study. Those who have attempted to find faculty positions have not been sought out or pursued. Those who have not yet entered the job market do not find themselves being pursued for positions. Indeed, many candidates in the sciences were quite concerned about finding jobs, and others had already left academe for industry because of their inability to find academic positions.

Myth three. The scholars represented in this study, both because of their competitive positioning in the market and their elite education, are only interested in being considered by the most prestigious institutions, making it virtually impossible for other institutions to recruit them.

Reality. Our participants describe a wide range of desired positions, regions of the country, institutional types, and kinds of teaching that they prefer. Some of these choices were based on limited mobility, while others were based on the environment the person wished to be in, a desire to teach a diverse student body, or the interest in joining an institution that had a mission related to the individual's professional goals. Indeed, it was not uncommon for our participants to express regret that they had not been recruited by a regional institution with which they had some affinity.

Myth four. Individuals are being continually recruited by wealthy and prestigious institutions with resources with which ordinary institutions cannot compete. This creates a revolving door that limits progress for any single institution in diversifying its faculty.

Reality. Some faculty do leave institutions and continue to be sought out, particularly those in the first and second prototypes. What emerged from the study, however, is the limited number of times that this had actually occurred and a greater understanding of the reasons behind the

The white men in the study regularly commented on the difficulty that persons who bring truly different perspectives (such as white women and faculty of color) have in being taken seriously on the job market

---

move when it did occur. Indeed, the notion that academics can and will pick up and move frequently simply because of monetary incentives is invariably not true. When people moved, the reasons often focused on unresolved issues with the institution, dual career choices, and whether the match was a good one, rather than on financial packages and institutional prestige. Thus, more often than not, people moved because of factors within the institution.

Myth five. Faculty of color are leaving academe altogether for more lucrative positions in government and industry.

Reality. We were able to include in our study those who have left academe for positions outside of higher education. Once again, the reasons for those choices focused on experiences within academic life. For scientists, a common explanation included the need to establish a career before the age of forty. The expectation of multiple postdoctoral appointments in the sciences often delayed academic career development. Others spoke of inhumane search processes that left them feeling unappreciated. Others noted the difficult job market. Thus, the choice to leave academe was as often a function of what was wrong with academe as it was of what was right outside.

Myth six. Campuses are so focused on diversifying the faculty that heterosexual white males have no chance on the academic labor market.

Reality. In our sample, it was clear that white males were slightly underrepresented in Prototype 1 and overrepresented in Prototype 6. Nevertheless, it is not the case that these men cannot find jobs. Indeed, combining Prototypes 1 and 2 revealed equivalent experiences on the job market. In most of the cases where white men had difficulty finding a regular faculty appointment, the fields in which they specialized had had virtually no openings. The vast majority, like the rest of those in the study, were also highly successful. Nevertheless, we observed two phenomena in the hiring experience related to these scholars. First, those who were in fields where there was little diversity, such as philosophy, described the continuing difficulty they observed for the relatively few white women and faculty of color. The white men in the study regularly commented on the difficulty that persons who bring truly different perspectives (such as white women and faculty of color) have in being taken seriously on the job market. That is, in these fields scholars who bring a different perspective still find it difficult to "break in." Being rare does not mean being sought out. The second pattern we observed is that these men who had introduced expertise related to diversity into the traditional discipline had a significant advantage on the job market. Thus, most of the white men in Prototype 1 offered diversity specializations within their discipline.

OTHER CONCLUSIONS

1. Because of the limited job market in many fields, campuses have sufficient choice among applicants to be able to raise the level of requirements for "qualified candidates." Institutions can raise their aspirations concerning the desirability of hiring candidates who attended the most elite institutions, have significant publications during doctoral work, and who have increased technical specialization. While our participants satisfied these criteria in many cases, many observed that other persons of color who are attending less elite institutions would be at a severe disadvantage. They also commented that these changes might not serve the institution, students, or higher education particularly well.

2. The search and hiring process continues largely unchanged. The results of this study suggests that while more and more administrators see the value of diversifying the faculties of American colleges and universities, faculty, particularly in some fields, are resistant to rethinking how they might recruit and evaluate candidates. The lack of diversity on search committees continues to limit the potential for introducing new perspectives to the process of evaluation.

3. There are particular strategies that graduate institutions can follow to encourage and nurture students in approaching the current academic market. From engaging new developments in the fields of scholarship to becoming involved professionally, students will need to be prepared to deal with what is clearly a difficult job market.

The future must be carefully negotiated in ways
that address the job market ethically but that
also continue to encourage graduate education
for students of color

4. Many institutions follow a rather passive approach to developing pools for the search process through letters and advertising. Successful searches require the development of personal connections, networks of people who are in advancing areas of scholarship, and a willingness to hire candidates for the perspectives that they bring, not just for the group they are supposed to represent.

5. Young scholars seek tenure-track positions as the primary goal of their searches and look to achieving tenure as a time when they can truly play a leadership role in their institutions by offering differing perspectives. The current discussions within higher education of alternatives to tenure raise potential problems for the attractiveness of higher education in the future.

6. The climate for faculty of color in institutions of higher education remains uncomfortable and difficult, no matter the circumstances under which the individual was hired. Thus, institutions that feel that they have made great efforts to hire someone may resent "the lack of appreciation," even as the scholar finds himself or herself not taken very seriously when an effort is made to participate in institutional change.

IMPLICATIONS

The current job market. This study raises some troubling questions for policy and practice. Because of the current tight job market, there are fewer opportunities for new faculty than had been predicted. As a result, many of the participants in this study were not always certain whether they would encourage faculty careers for others. The job market, the lack of opportunity, the climate on campus, the politics of higher education, and "inhumane" search processes were frequently cited. At the same time, the need to encourage scholars of color remains vitally important and is urgent. Indeed, if future candidates avoid academic careers then efforts at diversity will be even more significantly jeopardized than they are now. As changing demographics become more apparent in more parts of the country, the pressure to diversify the faculty will increase. At that point, some of the myths may indeed become realities. In light of this and in light of the continuing need to bring diverse perspectives to academe, the future must be carefully negotiated in ways that address the job market ethically but that also continue to encourage graduate education for students of color. At the present, the limited supply of faculty of color does not necessarily lead to unlimited opportunities; thus, future policy discussions will need to consider carefully the continuing predictions about the need for faculty in the future, the continuing need for a diverse faculty, and alternative ways to address these competing factors.

This issue is particularly important in the sciences, where postdoctoral fellowships do provide opportunities in a tight job market. The fact that postdoctoral work has now become a requirement of academic preparation for scientists is extremely troubling. It is certainly not clear that most institutions require another eight to ten years beyond the Ph.D. for the success of faculty. Moreover, it delays the development of serious careers, ratchets up the standards for what faculty will require of their institutions in order to continue their research once employed on a faculty, and makes it difficult for graduate students who cannot afford to delay entry into the profession from being considered seriously. While this is true for all science faculty, the differential impact on faculty of color, given their scarcity, is quite severe.

There is an emerging literature that examines the complexity of the problem. A recent study by Massy and Goldman (1995) suggests that simply increasing postdoctoral opportunities may only increase the demand for graduate students but does not address the demand for faculty. A study done for the Midwestern Higher Education Commission (Myers and Turner 1995) suggests that increasing all graduate study without differentially singling out scholars of color or white women in certain fields will have a negligible impact on diversifying the pool of candidates. Tobias, Cubin, and Aylesworth (1995) have suggested that for the sciences, at least, thinking more broadly about the nature of what one does with a Ph.D. and also thinking more critically about what talents are gong to be required will be a prerequisite for addressing the supply issues in science.

Opportunities for scholars of color will not necessarily
grow with the shifting job market unless there are
changes within institutional practice to complement
the change in the academic pipeline

Nevertheless, continuing analysis of future needs for faculty based on projected enrollments and faculty retirement seems to suggest that there will be a demand for faculty that requires the continuing development of scholars. This study suggests, however, that the opportunities for scholars of color will not necessarily grow with the shifting job market unless there are changes within institutional practice to complement the change in the academic pipeline.

Fellowships. Fellowship programs continue to be extraordinarily important. Not only do they provide financial support to pursue doctoral study, but they also emerge as important networking links and signs of legitimization. The Ford conferences, for example, represent a significant investment on the part of the Ford Foundation, but an investment that this study would suggest is well worth it. Indeed, one of the implications of this study is precisely that foundations might build in more opportunities for past and present recipients to network so that they might serve as champions for individuals when regular institutional practice is not as responsive as it might be.

The rhetoric of higher education. These data also suggest that the continuing rhetoric about "bidding wars" is not only false but damaging. While a limited job market restricts opportunities, it restricts opportunities for all. Moreover, in some cases, particularly where diversity is perceived to be irrelevant, the extreme competition restricts opportunity even more for scholars of color. To continue to perpetuate the myths of the pipeline damages the credibility of institutions and continues to divert the focus of institutional initiatives away from essential and required institutional changes.

Tenure. Emerging in the literature of higher education and in the discussions of national professional associations is the reconsideration of tenure. Often this issue is framed in ways that suggest a concern for creating openings for younger and more diverse faculties by creating the possibility of greater institutional flexibility in hiring. The results of this study would suggest that, quite to the contrary, tenure is often viewed by the scholars in our study as an important element precisely because of academic freedom issues. There were many comments that suggested that the difference in perspective often introduced by scholars of color and women is seen as a threat to the institution and, thus, often threatens the professional survival of those faculty members. Many of the individuals in our study viewed tenure as the opportunity to more fully contribute to and speak out about their intellectual, professional, and institutional obligations. Serious participation and informed data will need to be a part of any broad-based discussion about tenure, particularly as it relates to faculty diversity.

PRINCIPLES OF GOOD PRACTICE FOR HIRING INSTITUTIONS

While the focus of this study was not on institutional practices, the study did reveal some of the strategies, approaches, and attitudes which seemed to be the most effective.

Personal networking. Some institutions were named on a regular basis as having solicited applications from applicants of color. In some cases, the solicitations were no more than form letters asking for interest. These letters tended to be less powerful and often were ignored. Most effective were phone calls or personalized letters in which the search committee or administrator seemed to be familiar with the candidate's areas of interest and how these fit with the job description of the position.

In many cases, individuals on search committees had become familiar with the candidate and were instrumental in providing important links between the candidate and the institution. These connections were commonly developed at professional conferences, conferences like those sponsored by Ford, and through campus presentations and personal introductions. Indeed, one of the best strategies that institutions can develop is to support and encourage individual faculty members in developing networks among diverse communities of scholars. Institutions with past Ford fellows have a ready resource as long as these individuals are not overburdened with the responsibility for finding candidates. Moreover, many successful institutions began the process early, even before positions were available.

Leadership. Strong administrative action was often cited as a key element in a candidate being offered the position. In the long run, however, a close consensus between the search committee and the administration will be very important for the long-term success of the candidates. Often, candidates observed that many searches satisfied affirmative action requirements by diversifying the pool of those interviewed but that these were merely surface-level procedures—the institutions were not serious about hiring.

Commitment. The level of an institution's commitment to diversity is important for its credibility and for the seriousness with which candidates approach the institution. Scholars of all racial and ethnic backgrounds perceived that institutional efforts to diversify were "more talk than action." Many felt that without continuing pressure institutional efforts to achieve faculty diversity would decrease. Current efforts to diversify curricula and scholarship have created new areas of expertise for which faculty of color are more likely to be sought out.

Affirmative action for the right reasons. Our interviews indicate that affirmative action is supported with some ambivalence. People want to be hired for their scholarship abilities, not solely for their ethnicity. Many faculty of color had little respect or interest in those schools that sent out general mailings urging minorities or white women to apply. It was viewed by many as insulting and reflecting little genuine interest in the candidates themselves. At the same time, many spoke eloquently about the fear that the current backlash against affirmative action would reduce any institutional incentives to diversify and would work against future hiring and retention of faculty of color.

Championing. Searches were often effective because someone at the institution or on the search committee knew the candidate or got to know the candidate and served as a supporter in his or her job search.

Elitism. This study, while centered on those in elite institutions, highlights the need to examine carefully candidates' talents and achievements and not just their "pedigrees." Relying on traditional notions of quality will only serve to narrow the applicant pool and to narrow the range of talents that are brought to the search.

Dual-career issues. The challenge of dual-career relationships and dual-career academics was a common theme for these scholars as they approached the job market. It appeared, however, that many institutions are not prepared to assist candidates in dealing with the dual-career issue. In many cases, candidates were not expecting two appointments, although there were a few cases where a couple was offered two positions and took the offers. The perception was one of lack of interest or effort on the part of institutions. In the best cases, partners were aggressively assisted in finding positions or in connecting with possibilities in the area. Guaranteeing two positions is not necessarily in the best interest of the institution or fair to others. What appeared in many cases was that those campuses that were prepared to assist with partners and spouses were taken more seriously than those that left it up to the couple.

Posthiring support. Once hired, many respondents noted the need for help and support during their critical first years in the university. While all seemed to feel pressure from the heavy burden of preparing for a new class and trying to get a research program off the ground, women and minority members often experienced a disproportionately difficult burden associated with excessive committee assignments and student counseling. As several respondents emphasized, getting a job in the academy is only the first step. Succeeding in the multiple responsibilities of that job over the first seven years of the position in order to achieve tenure is a much more challenging proposition.

PRINCIPLES OF GOOD PRACTICE FOR GRADUATE INSTITUTIONS

In our interviews, we asked participants if they wished to send a message to the higher education community about their experiences on the job market. One of the most common themes had to do with limited opportunities for academic posts and what it is that graduate institutions should do to address this situation. Many, of course, suggested that graduate programs should limit or discontinue doctoral programs, particularly in fields where there were no openings. While this strategy has severe limitations, particularly given the erratic quality of the job market from year to year and

The most successful of our participants clearly pursued areas of interest related to diversity and found themselves experiencing a more vigorous job market than others

projections about the need for faculty in the future, a response must be developed which is ethical and honest about prevailing conditions.

Preparation. Many respondents urged graduate institutions to inform students early in their graduate careers about the realities of doctoral-level employment in their field. In addition, they suggested that graduate students should be given specific preparation in job search skills and in the management of the entire job search process in order to relieve the psychological stress that is experienced by many. Almost all of the participants, whether or not their job search was successful, mentioned that they wished they had known more about the search process and their prospects at the outset.

Career elitism. One of the lessons from these conversations was the narrowness in the perceptions of graduate faculty as to what kind of work and/or position is acceptable. Many of the participants commented that if they planned on pursuing a career other than a faculty position at a research university they were often not taken as seriously by their graduate faculty. It would appear that if graduate study is not to be curtailed, then considering broader sets of desirable options, from teaching at different kinds of institutions to other kinds of applied research, would be important. To do this well, graduate institutions will need to develop the networks and opportunities to make these choices a reality.

Changes in the fields. Many graduate students were not informed about how new developments in their fields were being incorporated into the changing college curricula of today. Thus, areas of study were often pursued independent of needs on college campuses. The most successful of our participants clearly pursued areas of interest related to diversity and found themselves experiencing a more vigorous job market than others. This was especially true in such fields as literature, history, and sociology. Graduate programs must be sensitive to emerging needs on college campuses, both from a scholarly and pedagogical perspective. Candidates that are prepared in these ways are more likely to experience greater success.

Championing. Championing the search was a powerful theme in this study. More often than expected, however, the champion proved to be someone in the hiring institution rather than in the graduate institution. The most successful graduate programs were ones where individual relationships and departmental programs were available to provide the graduate student with support in preparing for the job market. The most exemplary programs helped students prepare for interviews, encouraged and even required presentations at conferences, provided support for publishing during the doctoral program, and were especially aggressive in helping students network. Students who had champions were much more likely to be successful in finding a desirable position.

FUTURE STUDY

The complexity of the relationships among the numerous factors that will affect the development and future strength of the American professoriate requires systematic and interdisciplinary study. Supply and demand issues, we now know, cannot be assumed to affect all young professionals in the same way. Disciplinary variations, retirement policies, state funding, national support for research, technological changes, and curricular shifts in colleges and universities are all having an impact. Negotiating this shifting terrain requires something more than econometric models and will require the kind of interdisciplinary study and introduction of multiple perspectives not often seen in academic policy research.

CONCLUSION

There is a clear disjuncture between prevailing perceptions in the literature and among institutions of higher education concerning the academic pipeline, the job market, and the perceptions of our participants. We know that if every institution were seriously trying to diversify, there would not be enough diversity in the academic pipeline. That does not mean that everyone, or even most people, is having an easy time being hired or being taken seriously. The disparity between institutional rhetoric and individual experiences aggravates an already difficult situation.

> What is imperative is that institutions must not
> fall back on the myths—they are untrue, they are
> damaging, and they misname the problem and the
> potential solutions

The mutually contradictory perceptions—the supply and under-supply arguments—are alive and well and are, to only a modest degree, simultaneously true. There are some faculty who are sought out and who can negotiate their positions, but there are also many more for whom a single offer was typical. Moreover, in the sciences we see a troubling and wasteful use of talent. Multiple postdoctoral fellowships have now raised the years of training and technical skills for faculty, most of whom will not end up teaching at research universities where such skills would be essential. The current myths do great damage and weaken the integrity of institutional efforts at hiring as well. They leave open the genuine possibility that in all too many cases, the rhetoric of diversity is just that. At the same time, it is clear that the current job market makes the strategies for hiring and the strategies for continuing to encourage diverse groups of people to enter academe quite complicated and troubling. What is imperative is that institutions must not fall back on the myths—they are untrue, they are damaging, and they misname the problem and the potential solutions. Indeed, they create a self-fulfilling prophecy. Moreover, the implications of the current economy of higher education are dangerous even for sincere efforts at diversifying the American faculty, let alone for the development of the new faculty of the future of all backgrounds. To resolve this issue, with its profound implications for the nation, will require not merely single institutional approaches, but also the combined efforts of policymakers in higher education, fellowship programs, and scholars.

Bibliography

Adams, H. G. 1988. Tomorrow's professoriate: Insuring minority participation through talent development today. Paper presented at the Engineering Deans Council Student Pipeline Workshop, American Society for Engineering Education, Washington, D.C.

Almost no blacks in the natural sciences at the nation's highest ranked universities. 1994/1995. *The Journal of Blacks in Higher Education* 6: 14–16.

Blackwell, J. E. 1988. Faculty issues: The impact on minorities. *The Review of Higher Education* 2 (4): 417–434.

Bowen, H. R., and J. H. Schuster. 1986. *American professors: A national resource imperiled.* New York: Oxford University Press.

Bowen, W. G., and J. A. Sosa. 1989. *Prospects for faculty in the arts and sciences: A study of factors affecting demand and supply, 1987–2012.* Princeton: Princeton University Press.

Bronstein, P., E. D. Rothblum, and S. E. Solomon. 1993. Ivy halls and glass walls: Barriers to academic careers for women and ethnic minorities. *New Directions for Institutional Learning* 53: 17–31.

Brown, S. V., B. C. Clewell, R. B. Ekstrom, and D. E. Powers. 1994. *Research agenda for the Graduate Record Examinations Board minority graduate education project: An update.* Princeton: Educational Testing Service.

California Postsecondary Education Commission. 1990. *Planning for a new faculty: Issues for the twenty-first century.* Sacramento: California Postsecondary Education Commission.

Carter, D. J., and E. M. O'Brien. 1993. Employment and hiring patterns for faculty of color. *Research Briefs* 4: 6. Washington, D.C.: Division of Policy Analysis and Research, American Council on Education.

Carter, D. J., and R. R. Wilson. 1994. *Minorities in higher education: Thirteenth annual status report.* Washington, D.C.: American Council on Education.

Clotfelter, C. T., R. G. Ehrenberg, M. Getz, and J. J. Siegfried, eds. 1991. *Economic challenges in higher education.* Chicago: University of Chicago Press.

Collins, R. W., and J. A. Johnson. 1990. One institution's success in increasing the number of minority faculty: A provost's perspective. *Peabody Journal of Education* 66 (1): 71–76.

Cross, T. 1994. Black faculty at Harvard: Does the pipeline defense hold water? *The Journal of Blacks in Higher Education* 4: 42–46.

de la Luz Reyes, M., and J. J. Halcon. 1991. Practices of the academy: Barriers to access for Chicano academics. In *The racial crisis in American higher education*, edited by P. G. Altbach and K. Lomotey. Albany: State University of New York Press.

El-Khawas, E. 1988. *Campus Trends, 1988*. Higher Education Panel Reports, no. 78. Washington, D.C.: American Council on Education.

———. 1990. *Campus Trends, 1990*. Higher Education Panel Reports, no. 80. Washington, D.C.: American Council on Education.

Garza, H. 1988. The barrioization of Hispanic faculty. *Educational Record* 68 (4): 122–24.

———. 1992. Academic power, discourse, and legitimacy: Minority scholars in U.S. universities. In *Community empowerment and Chicano scholarship*, edited by M. Romero and C. Candelaria. Houston, Tex.: National Association for Chicano Studies.

Golladay, M. A. 1989. Women and minority faculty in engineering: Reviewing the figures. *Engineering Education* 74 (5): 573–76.

Harvey, W. B., and D. Scott-Jones. 1985. We can't find any: The elusiveness of black faculty members in American higher education. *Issues in Education* 3: 68–76.

Ivey, E. 1988. Recruiting more women into engineering and science. *Engineering Education* 78 (8): 762–65.

Massy, W. F., and C. A. Goldman. 1995. *The production and utilization of science and engineering doctorates in the United States*. Stanford, Calif.: Stanford Institute for Higher Education Research.

Menges, R. J., and W. H. Exum. 1983. Barriers to the progress of women and minority faculty. *Journal of Higher Education* 54 (2): 122–143.

Michelson, R. A., and M. L. Oliver. 1991. Making the short list: Black candidates and the faculty recruitment process. In *The racial crisis in American higher education*, edited by P. G. Altbach and K. Lomotey. Albany: State University of New York Press.

Mooney, C. J. 1989. Affirmative action goals, coupled with tiny number of minority Ph.D.'s, set off faculty recruiting frenzy. *Chronicle of Higher Education*, 2 August, p. A10.

Moore, W., Jr. 1988. Black faculty in white colleges: A dream deferred. *Educational Record* (fall/winter): 117–121.

Myers, S. L., Jr., and C. S. V. Turner. 1995. Minority faculty development project. Midwestern Higher Education Commission, Minneapolis.

National Center for Education Statistics. 1992. *Digest of educational statistics.* Washington, D.C.: National Center for Education Statistics, U.S. Department of Education.

National Research Council. 1991. *Summary report 1990: Doctorate recipients from United States universities.* Washington, D.C.: National Academy Press.

National Science Foundation. 1994. *Characteristics of doctoral scientists and engineers in the United States: 1991.* Arlington, Va.: National Science Foundation.

Norrell, S. A., and J. I. Gill. 1991. *Bringing into focus the factors affecting faculty supply and demand: A primer for higher education and state policymakers.* Boulder, Colo.: Western Interstate Commission for Higher Education.

Olivas, M. A. 1988. Latino faculty at the border. Increasing numbers key to more Hispanic access. *Change* 20 (3): 6–9.

Opp, R. E., and A. Smith. 1994. Effective strategies for enhancing minority faculty recruitment. *Community College Journal of Research and Practice* 10: 147.

Ottinger, C., R. Sikula, and C. Washington. 1993. Production of minority doctorates. *Research Briefs* 4: 8. Washington, D.C.: Division of Policy Analysis and Research, American Council on Education.

Russell, S. 1991. The status of women and minorities in higher education: Findings from the 1987 national survey of postsecondary faculty. *CUPA Journal* 42: 1.

Sandler, B. R. 1986. *The campus climate revisited: Chilly for women faculty, administrators, and graduate students.* Washington, D.C.: Association of American Colleges.

Schapiro, M. O., M. P. O'Malley, and L. H. Litten. 1991. Progression to graduate school from the elite colleges and universities. *Economics of Education Review* 10 (3): 227–244.

Schuster, J. H. 1992. Academic labor markets. In vol. 3 of *The Encyclopedia of Higher Education,* edited by B. R. Clark and G. R. Neave. Oxford, Tarrytown, N.Y.: Pergamon Press.

Shoemaker, E. A., and R. L. McKeen. 1975. Affirmative action and hiring practices in higher education. *Research in Higher Education* 3: 359–364.

Smith, D. G. 1989. *The challenge of diversity: Involvement or alienation in the academy?* Washington, D.C.: School of Education and Human Development, George Washington University.

Solorzano, D. G. 1993. *The road to the doctorate for California's Chicanas and Chicanos: A study of Ford Foundation minority fellows.* Berkeley: California Policy Seminar.

Staples, R. 1984. Racial ideology and intellectual racism: Blacks in academia. *Black Scholar* 15: 2–17.

Strober, M. H., et al. 1993. *Report of the provost's committee on the recruitment and retention of women faculty.* Stanford, Calif.: Stanford University.

Suinn, R. M., and J. C. Witt. 1982. Survey on ethnic minority faculty recruitment and retention. *American Psychologist* 37 (11): 1239–1244.

Swoboda, M. J. 1993. Hiring women and minorities. In *The art of hiring in America's colleges and universities*, edited by R. H. Stein and S. J. Trachtenberg. Buffalo, N.Y.: Prometheus Books.

Tobias, S., D. E. Cubin, and K. Aylesworth. 1995. *Rethinking science as a career: Perceptions and realities in the physical sciences.* Tucson, Ariz.: Research Corporation.

Thurgood, D. H., and J. E. Clarke. 1995. *Doctorate recipients from United States universities: Summary report 1993.* Washington, D.C.: Doctorate Records Project, National Research Council.

Washington, V., and W. Harvey. 1989. *Affirmative rhetoric, negative action: African American and Hispanic faculty at predominantly white institutions.* Washington, D.C.: School of Education and Human Development, George Washington University.

White, J. A. 1989. The engineering faculty pipeline: An NSF perspective. *Engineering Education,* 79 (5): 547–49.

White, P. E. 1992. *Women and minorities in science and engineering: An update.* Washington, D.C.: National Science Foundation.

Wilson, R. 1987. Recruitment and retention of minority faculty and staff. *AAHE Bulletin* (February): 11–14.

———. 1995. Hiring of black scholars stalls at some major universities. *Chronicle of Higher Education,* 2 June, p. A16.

————. 1995. Finders, keepers? Recruiting—and retaining—minority faculty members challenges Old Dominion University. *Chronicle of Higher Education*, 2 June, p. A13

Yale University. 1990. Report on the committee on recruitment and retention of minority group members on the faculty at Yale. *Minerva* 28 (2): 217–47.

The Association of American Colleges and Universities is the only institutional-membership higher education association whose primary mission is promoting liberal education. AAC&U strives to strengthen undergraduate curricula and revitalize classroom teaching and learning through research and development projects, publications, national and regional meetings and workshops, and multicampus partnerships and networks.

Founded in 1915, AAC&U comprises public and private colleges and universities of all types and sizes. AAC&U's activities build bridges across disciplines and forge links between administrators, academic leaders, and faculty members. By creating a national community of purposes among institutions that share a concern for how undergraduates are taught and what they learn, AAC&U influences higher education's responses to the full range of today's academic challenges.